CAMBRIDGE LIBRARY COLLECTION

Books of enduring scholarly value

Printing and Publishing History

The interface between authors and their readers is a fascinating subject in its own right, revealing a great deal about social attitudes, technological progress, aesthetic values, fashionable interests, political positions, economic constraints, and individual personalities. This part of the Cambridge Library Collection reissues classic studies in the area of printing and publishing history that shed light on developments in typography and book design, printing and binding, the rise and fall of publishing houses and periodicals, and the roles of authors and illustrators. It documents the ebb and flow of the book trade supplying a wide range of customers with products from almanacs to novels, bibles to erotica, and poetry to statistics.

Bibliotheca Ratcliffiana

The library of the chandler John Ratcliffe (1707–76) was amassed before the onset of 'bibliomania', and perfectly illustrates the last days of a period of book collecting when scholars and commoners could hope to compete with wealthy noblemen. The collection contained over a hundred incunabula, including forty-eight Caxtons, and a fine selection of sixteenth-century English books, alongside contemporary literature and Presbyterian tracts. Many of Ratcliffe's incunabula had been purchased from James West, others from Anthony Askew. In turn, his books were acquired by a circle of his contemporaries, including William Herbert, Charles Chauncy and William Hunter. However, the purchase of some of the finest books by the aristocratic Justin MacCarthy Reagh provided a hint of what was to come. Reissued here is James Christie's 1776 sale catalogue, featuring handwritten annotations by an attendee at the auction who recorded the prices paid and the names of buyers.

T0349135

Cambridge University Press has long been a pioneer in the reissuing of out-of-print titles from its own backlist, producing digital reprints of books that are still sought after by scholars and students but could not be reprinted economically using traditional technology. The Cambridge Library Collection extends this activity to a wider range of books which are still of importance to researchers and professionals, either for the source material they contain, or as landmarks in the history of their academic discipline.

Drawing from the world-renowned collections in the Cambridge University Library and other partner libraries, and guided by the advice of experts in each subject area, Cambridge University Press is using state-of-the-art scanning machines in its own Printing House to capture the content of each book selected for inclusion. The files are processed to give a consistently clear, crisp image, and the books finished to the high quality standard for which the Press is recognised around the world. The latest print-on-demand technology ensures that the books will remain available indefinitely, and that orders for single or multiple copies can quickly be supplied.

The Cambridge Library Collection brings back to life books of enduring scholarly value (including out-of-copyright works originally issued by other publishers) across a wide range of disciplines in the humanities and social sciences and in science and technology.

Bibliotheca Ratcliffiana

*A Catalogue of the Elegant
and Truly Valuable Library of John Ratcliffe*

JAMES CHRISTIE

CAMBRIDGE
UNIVERSITY PRESS

CAMBRIDGE
UNIVERSITY PRESS

University Printing House, Cambridge, CB2 8BS, United Kingdom

Published in the United States of America by Cambridge University Press, New York

Cambridge University Press is part of the University of Cambridge.

It furthers the University's mission by disseminating knowledge in the pursuit of
education, learning and research at the highest international levels of excellence.

www.cambridge.org
Information on this title: www.cambridge.org/9781108065825

© in this compilation Cambridge University Press 2014

This edition first published 1776
This digitally printed version 2014

ISBN 978-1-108-06582-5 Paperback

Selected books of related interest, also reissued in the
CAMBRIDGE LIBRARY COLLECTION

Anonymous: *Catalogue of the Valuable Library of the Late Rev. Henry Richards Luard* (1891) [ISBN 9781108057295]

Baker and Leigh: *Bibliotheca Askeviana* (1774–84) [ISBN 9781108065849]

Bodleian Library: *A Catalogue of the Books Relating to British Topography, and Saxon and Northern Literature* (1814) [ISBN 9781108057318]

Christie, James: *Bibliotheca Ratcliffiana* (1776) [ISBN 9781108065825]

Clark, John Willis: *The Care of Books* (1902) [ISBN 9781108005081]

Curwen, Henry: *A History of Booksellers* (1874) [ISBN 9781108021432]

Dee, John, edited by James Orchard Halliwell, James Crossley, John Eglington Bailey and M.R. James: *John Dee's Diary, Catalogue of Manuscripts and Selected Letters* (1842, 1851, 1880, 1921) [ISBN 9781108050562]

Dibdin, Thomas Frognall: *Bibliomania* (1811) [ISBN 9781108015806]

Dibdin, Thomas Frognall: *Bibliophobia* (1832) [ISBN 9781108015592]

Dibdin, Thomas Frognall: *Bibliotheca Spenceriana* (4 vols., 1814–15) [ISBN 9781108051118]

Dibdin, Thomas Frognall: *Reminiscences of a Literary Life* (2 vols., 1836) [ISBN 9781108009355]

Duff, E. Gordon: *A Century of the English Book Trade* (1905) [ISBN 9781108026765]

Duff, E. Gordon: *Early Printed Books* (1893) [ISBN 9781108026741]

Edwards, Edward: *Free Town Libraries, their Formation, Management, and History* (1869) [ISBN 9781108009362]

Edwards, Edward: *Libraries and Founders of Libraries* (1864) [ISBN 9781108010528]

Edwards, Edward: *Memoirs of Libraries* (3 vols., 1859) [ISBN 9781108010566]

Evans, Robert Harding: *A Catalogue of the Library of the Late John, Duke of Roxburghe* (1812) [ISBN 9781108065832]

Evans, Robert Harding: *White Knights Library* (1819) [ISBN 9781108065986]

Fagan, Louis: *The Life of Sir Anthony Panizzi, K.C.B.* (2 vols., 1880) [ISBN 9781108044912]

King, Thomas: *Bibliotheca Farmeriana* (1798) [ISBN 9781108065993]

Oates, J.C.T.: *Catalogue of the Fifteenth-Century Printed Books in the University Library, Cambridge* (2 vols., 1954) [ISBN 9781108008488]

Sayle, C.E.: *Early English Printed Books in the University Library, Cambridge* (4 vols., 1900–7) [ISBN 9781108007818]

Wheatley, Henry Benjamin: *How to Form a Library* (1886) [ISBN 9781108021494]

Wheatley, Henry Benjamin: *How to Catalogue a Library* (1889) [ISBN 9781108021487]

For a complete list of titles in the Cambridge Library Collection please visit:
www.cambridge.org/features/CambridgeLibraryCollection/books.htm

Bibliotheca Ratcliffiana.

A
C A T A L O G U E
Of the Elegant and truly Valuable
L I B R A R Y
Of *J O H N R A T C L I F F E*, Efq;
Late of *B E R M O N D S E Y*,
D E C E A S E D,

The Whole collected with great Judgment and Expence
during the laft thirty Years of his Life ;

Comprehending the largeft and moft choice Collection of the rare old
Englifh Black Letter, in fine Prefervation and in elegant Bindings,
printed by Caxton, Lettou, Machlinia, the anonymous St. Alban's
Schoolmafter, Wynkyn de Worde, Pynfon, Berthelet, Grafton, Day,
Newberie, Marfhe, Jugge, Whytchurch, Wyer, R ftell, Coplande,
and the Reft of the Old Englifh Typographers; feveral Miffals and
MSS. and two Pedigrees on Vellum, finely illuminated ;

Amongft which are the following VALUABLE and SCARCE
BOOKS, *viz.*

Chaucer, 1ft Edit.	The Proud Lady, 1485,
Game of Cheffe,	Hyftorie of Roberte the Dyvell,
The Praife of Women,	Myrrour of the World,
Godefrey of Boleyne,	Tulle of old Age,
Gower, Confeffio Amantis,	Doctrine of Sapyence,
Legenda Aurea,	Kalendayr of Shypars,
The Wydow Edyth,	Orcharde of Syone,
The Cyte of Ladyes,	Pilgrimage of Perfection,
Lyfe of St. Catherine,	Lyfe of our Lady,
Lyfe of St. Wenefrede,	Cuftomes of London,
Reynard the Fox,	The Boke called Caton,
Sayenges of Philofophers,	Polychronicon, 2 Copies,
Hyftory of Prince and King Arthur,	Booke for a Kynge,
Dives and Pauper,	Snyppe of Foles.
The Dyinge Creature,	Boke of Dyftyllacyon, &c. &c.
Dyftruccyon of Troye,	

Chronicles by Caxton, Raftell, Boece, Froffart, Grafton, Hall, Fabian,
Hollinfhed, Speed, Stow, Mundy, Cooper, Hardyng, &c. &c.
Chambers's Dictionary, 2 Vols. Harris's Voyages, 2 Vols. Gerard's
Herbal, 2 Vols. coloured, Atkins's Gloucefterfhire, Mr. Walpole's
Pieces, Morocco, Pope's works, 5 Vols. L. P. Granger's Biography,
4 Vols. Ames's Printing, Puritan Tracts, 20 Vols. Morocco, Politi-
cal State, 60 Vols. Morocco, with many others equally good.

Which will be Sold by AUCTION.
By Mr. *C H R I S T I E,*

At his Great Room, the *Royal A ademy*, Pall Mall,
On *Wednefday, March* 27. 1776 and the 8 following Even-
ings (Good Friday and Sunday excepted)
To be viewed on Monday the 25th, and to the Time of Sale, which
will begin each Evening at Six o'Clock.
Catalogues may be then had at the Place of Sale, and at the Bank and
Garraway's Coffee Houfes

⁎ Mr. Ratcliffe's curious Manfcript Catalogues will be fold in the
laft Day's Sale.

1776

Explicationes Literarum Capitalium, &ç.

M.	-	Morocco.
C. R.	-	Corio Ruffico.
C. T.	-	Corio Turcico.
M. B.	-	Morocco Back.
G. L.	-	Gilt Leaves.
L. P.	-	Large Paper.
R. 'r.	-	Ruled.

A Catalogue, &c.

First Day's Sale,

WEDNESDAY, MARCH 27, 1776.

PAMPHLETS.

		£	s.	d.
1	SIX bundles of sermons	—	10	6
2	four ditto, by eminent diffenters	—	5	6
3	three ditto, funeral	—	11	—
4	three ditto, various	—	7	—
5	feven ditto, before the fons of the clergy, &c.	—	3	6
6	eight ditto, 30th of January, affizes, fafts, &c.	—	6	—
7	one ditto, moftly black letter	—	9	—
8	one ditto, preached before 1640	—	5	6
9	two bundles of catalogues, one ditto, very curious	—	8	—
10	56 plays, 12mo	—	11	—
11	33 plays, operas, farces, &c.	—	6	6
12	14 plays, 8vo.	—	16	—
13	42 ditto, 4to.	—	10	—
14	five bundles of gentleman, polite and grand magazines, &c.	—	17	—
15	56, poetry mifcellaneous	—	5	—
16	54, beft poetry	—	7	—
17	100, curious and entertaining	—	12	6

£. s. d

7. 13. 6

Collins —. 3. – 18 54, 4to. moſtly political poetry
Do —. 3. – 19 53, 4to. miſcellaneous
—. 3. – 20 45, 4to. miſcellaneous
—. 10.621 67, 4to. moſtly modern, curious, odd and diverting
—. 4. –22 100, fol. poetry miſcellaneous
—. 4. –23 2:, 8vo. hiſtorical and entertaining
—. 16.624 94, 8vo. &c. phyſical

OCTAVO & DUODECIMO.

—. 8. – 25 Featley's fountain of tears, Boyle's tracts, and 25 more
—. 8. 626 Hale's contemplations, Bunyan's holy war, and 34 more
—. 7. 627 Howe on delighting in God, and 36 more
—. 7. – 28 Sandys's divine poems, and 8 more, morocco, gilt leaves
—. 9. – 29 Morton's New-England's memorial. 1721, Blome's deſcription of Jamaica, 1672, and 28 more
—. 9. – 30 Athenian ſpy, tale of a tub, and 35 more
—. 4. 631 Paries' method of caring gun-ſhotwounds, by Hamond, 1617, and 11 more
—. 3. – 32 avantures de Telemaque, and 17 more
—. 5. 633 Ciceronis academ. queſt. apud Colinæum, 1535, and 15 more
—. 2. 63 t la philoſophe du bon ſens, par D'Argens, and 7 more
—. 3. – 35 Metamorphoſes D'Ovide, avec fig. and 6 more
—. 5. 6 36 Verſtegan's antiquities, 1655, Herne's account of the Charter-houſe, Gaffarel's unheard of curioſities, by Chilmead, 1650
—. 2. – 37 Du Verney's treatiſe of hearing, and 5 more
—. 8. – 38 Lawrence's chriſtian prudence, and 37 more
—. 4. – 39 Cotton's poetical works, 1689, and 5 more
—. 5. – 40 the art how to know men, 1665, and 11 more
—. 6. – 41 Toland's pieces, 8 v. 1726, &c.
—. 4. 642 Jurieu s chriſtian devotion, and 5 more, red morocco
—. 5. – 43 Connor's hiſtory of Poland, 2 v. 1698, and 6 more
—. 2. – 45 Leſtrange's hiſtory of the times, 1687, 1. p. c. t.
—. 4. 645 Burnet's ſtate of the dead, by Earbery, 2 v. 1728, and 4 more
—. 7. – 46 Fogg's weekly journal, letters, &c. 2 v. and 9 more
—. 5. 647 Biſhop Burnet's hiſtory of the reformation, cuts, and 5 more
—. 9. – 48 Taylor's contemplations, and 12 more

16. 6. 9

49 Winftanley's loyal martyrology, with their portraits, — . 5 . —
and 7 more
50 London and Wife's complete gardener, and 2 more — . 2. 6
51 Barton's analogy of divine wifdom, and 5 more — . 3 . —
52 Patrick's witneffes to chriftianity, and 11 more — . 4. 6
53 Whifton's aftronomical principles of religion, and 11 — . 5. 9
more
54 Bennet's chriftian oratory and 2 more — . 3. 6
55 collection of funeral fermons 2 v. Leighton's fermons — . 5 . —
56 Hildrop's free thoughts on the brute creation and 8 — . 4 . —
more
57 the life of a fatyrical puppy called Nim ; with two curi- — . 3. —Thane
ous port raits
58 Trebeck's fermons, and 9 more — . 4. —
59 avantures de Robinfon Crufoe, 3 t. avec fig. Am. 1727 — . 5. —Mc.Can
œuvres de Creffet, 2 t.   Lond. 1750
60 the independent whig, 3 v.   1725 — . 4. 6
61 adventures of Jofeph Andrews. 2 v. beauties of the En- — . 6. 6
glifh ftage, 2 v.
62 Homer's iliad, 5 v. by Dacier with Coypell's cuts 1712 — . 9. 6
63 Barron's cordial for low fpirits, a collection of valu- — . 6. —
able tracts, 3 v. 1751, the pillars of Prieftcraft,
and Orthodoxy fhaken, 2 v.   1752
64 Shakefpeare's works with the gloffary, 9 v.   1747 — . 18. —
65 the guardian and freeholder, 3 v.   1740 — . 5. —
66 fpectator, 8 v. m. g. l.   1739 1. 5. —
67 Turkifh Spy, 9 v   1730 — . 17. —
68 Skinner's life of General Monk, l. p.   1723 — . 3. —
69 Lewis's life of Caxton the firft Englifh printer, l. p. — . 11. —
1737, Collin's life of Lord Burghley   1732
70 memoirs of the life and writings of Mr. Whifton, 3 v. — . 3. 6
1749
71 Mottley's life of Peter the great, 3 v. l. p. m. g. l. 1. 12. —
1739
72 Oppian's halieuticks by Jones, l. p. m. g. l. Ox. 1722 — . 12. —Payne
73 collection of occafional papers, for the year 1716, 3 v. — . 6. 6
74 Warburton's divine legation of Mofes, 3 v.   1738 — . 5. 6
75 Izacke's antiquities of the city of Exeter, m. g. l. 1724 — . 3. —
76 Emlyn's works, 3 v. neat   1746 — . 6. —
77 Crofby's hiftory of the Englifh baptifts, 4 v. 1738 — . 9. —Crofby.
78 a collection of poetry from the beft authors, 4 v. — . 7. 6
79 the free-thinker, 3 v. l. p. a fine fet, 1722 — . 6. 6
80 the tatler, 4 v. l. p. not uniform   1710 — . 9. —
81 the gentleman's magazine, 1731 to 1750, incl. 20 v. neat 3. 4. —Thane

£. s. d
32 . 6. 6

16. 6 82 The life of Henry Welby, Efq; who lived at his houfe in Grub-ftreet 44 years, and in that fpace was never feen by any, aged 84 (with his portrait) very fcarce, 1637

Fox. —. 4. — 83 Kilburn's furvey of Kent 1659

—. 17. — 84 curious tracts, viz. Afcham's fchole of fhooting, bl. l. 1571, Digbies' art of fwimming, by Middleton, cuts, bl. l. 1595, a booke of fifhinge with hooke and lyne, cuts, bl. l. 1600, the arte of planting and graftinge, bl. l. cuts 1589, Silver's paradoxes of defence, cuts 1599, Browne's arte of riding the Great horfe, cuts 1628, Cooke's perfpective glaffe of warre, 1628, Neade's double-armed man, fhewing the ufe of the long bowe and fpike, cuts 1625

—. 6. — 85 Sir John Davies's poems, 1603, Alexis's fecretes, by Warde, bl. l. London, printed by Hall 1562

1. 5. — 86 protraictures of the kings of England, 1597, lyfe of the bleffed martyr St. Thomas, bl. l. the boke of the lyfe and deth of Virgilius, bl. l. cronicle of warre of Salufte, by Thonas Paynell, bl. l. 1557, and 2 more

—. 5. — 87 Goodman's penitent pardon'd, cuts, and 11 more

— 6. — 88 holy Bible, imperfect, and 11 more

— 9. — 89 collection of mifcellaneous tracts, 8 v.

—. 3. 6 90 Darcie's annals of Queen Elizabeth, 1615, hiftory of firft fourteen years of James I, and 2 more

—. 2. 6 91 Bacon's letters, by Stephens, and 3 more

—. 4. — 92 the holy Bible, bl. let. 1586, and 6 more

—. 3. 6 93 Prynne's players fcourge, 1633, killing no murder, by Allen, and one more

Man. —. 5. 6 94 Story's hiftory of the wars of Ireland, 1693, Hackluyt's hiftory of the Weft-Indies, by Lok, and 3 more

—. 14. 6 95 Harcourt's relation of a voyage to Guiana, 1613, Poyntz's profpect of Tobago, 1683, Plantaganet's defcription of New Albion, &c. 1648, and two more

—. 4. — 96 Camus's admirable events, 1639, and 2 more

—. 3. 6 97 Northbrooke's treatife of dicing, dancing, plaies, idle paftimes, &c. imp. by Dawfon, bl. l. 1579, and one more

Carter —. 2. 6 98 Saunder's fupper of our Lord, bl. l. Lovanii, 1566, and 3 more

£. s. d

38. 18. 6

FOLIO.

£. s. d
55. 3.

—. 5. 6 125 Ligon's hiftory of Barbadoes, morocco back, g. l. 1673
           Ludolphus's hiftory of Ethiopia, cuts bad con. 1682

—. 6. 6 126 Grimefton's hiftory of France and Spain, 2 v.   1611

—. 11. — 127 ———— imperial hiftory and hiftory of the Netherlands,
           2 v.   1608

—. 3. 6 128 Spotfwood's hiftory of the church of Scotland, with
           his head, and one more

—. 8. — 129 Ware's hiftory and antiquities of Ireland, 1705, Lloyd's
           lives of eminent perfons   1668

—. 13. — 130 Weever's ancient funeral monuments, head and index,
           a fine copy   1631

—. 17. — 131 Plinie's natural hiftory, by Holland, a fine copy 1601

—. 16. — 132 Maitland's hiftory of Edinburgh, cuts   1753

Thane. —. 15. — 133 Drayton's Poly Albion, cuts

—. 8. 6 134 Wither's collection of emblems, with his portr. 1635

—. 4. 6 135 les hiftoires d'Herodote, par Du-Ruyer, m. g. l.
                        Par. 1658

Thane 1. 2. — 136 Leigh's natural hiftory of Lancafhire, Chefhire, &c.
           cuts, a fine copy   1700

Cater 1. 1. — 137 Atkyns's ancient and prefent ftate of Gloucefterfhire,
           cuts, half bound, l. p.   1765

D?   —. 7. — 138 Gwillim's difplay of heraldry, 5th edit.   1679

  3. 17. — 139 the Holy Bible, cuts, C. R. G. L. R. Camb. by
           Field   1660

  1. 5. — 140 Bowen's complete fyftem of geography, 2 v.   1747

  2. 4. — 141 Coetlogon's hiftory of Arts and fciences, 2 v. cuts,
           neat   1745

—. 10. 6 142 Chaucer's works, bl. l. a fair copy, printed by Iflip,
                           1602

—. 14. 6 143 Stow's chronicle of England, bl. l. fair   1615

—. 8. — 144 Grafton's chronicle of England, bl. l. one leaf want-
           ing   1568

W   2. —. — 145 heir beginnis the hiftory and chronicles of Scotland,
           by Mafter Hector Boece, 1541, very fair

—. 13. 6 146 Holinfhed's chronicles of England, Scotland and
           Ireland, bl. l. 2 v. in 1, very fair   1586

£ —. 12. — 147 Archbifhop Cranmer's Bible, 2 v. b. l.

£ 74. 17. 0

End of the Firft Day's Sale.

Second Day's Sale,

THURSDAY, MARCH 28, 1776.

Pamphlets.

£. s. d

148	TWO bundles of lives, trials, pirates, &c.	1.4.
149	one ditto of lives, memoirs of ministers and pr ests of all sorts	_.6.6 Chapman
150	three ditto relating to orator Henley, Bolingbroke and the Jews	– .5. _ Hayes
151	one ditto on religious subjects	__ _ _ _ _.6. _ Harwood
152	three ditto on trade, coin, bank, America, &c.	_ _ _.18. _ Nichols
153	one ditto relating to marriage	_ _ _ - _.5. _
154	three ditto to dissenters for and against	_ _ _ _.11. _
155	one ditto lives, Will's memoirs, &c. regal and noble	_.8.6 Nichols
156	three ditto on deism, schism and earthquakes	_ _ _.4. _ Chapman
157	three ditto extraordinary conversions, religious, odd and strange, miscellaneous, &c.	_.13.6 Dᵇ
158	one ditto methodists, moravians and opponents	_ _ 3. _ Hayes
159	three bundles in the reigns of King William, Queen Ann, and George 1st	_ .6. _ Nichols
160	four ditto by Palmer, Millar, Asgill, White, Towgood, &c. &c.	_ .2.6 Roby.
161	three ditto miscellaneous, trinitarian, &c. &c.	_ _ 2.6 Harwood
162	three ditto satyrical on the clergy, medicinal, magazines, &c.	_.6.6 W.
163	two ditto by Watts and Chandler	.7.6 Roby.
164	five ditto bangorian controversy, &c. &c.	_.2.6
165	two ditto by Dr. Clarke and opponents, &c.	_.3._ Harwood
166	Akinside's pleasures of imagination, and 19 more, poetry	_.4.6

B

Nichols—. 15. _ 167 one bundle relating to the colonies, &c.

—. 3. 6 168 Farmer's effay on the learning of Shakespear, and fix more

—. 3. _ 169 Miller's account of the univerfity of Cambridge, and 14 more

D? —. 3. _ 170 Bp. Warburton's enquiry into the caufes of prodigies and miracles   1727

—. 4. 6 171 Ames's catalogue of Englifh heads   1748

—. 2. _ 172 Philemon to Hydafpes, by Mr. Coventry, 5 parts, compt.

OCTAVO & DUODECIMO.

Chapman—. 5. _ 173 Sacheverel's account of the Ifle of man, 1702, and 29 more

—. 4. 6 174 King's heathen gods, and 5 more

—. 2. 6 175 Waller's poems, fm: edit. 1712, and 3 more

—. 5. 6 176 Potter's antiquities of Greece, 2 v. 1767, and 1 more

—. 2. 6 177 Pomfret's poems, and 5 more

—. 2. _ 178 Manwaring's account of the claffic authors, and 6 more

—. 3. 6 179 the old whig, or the confiftent proteftant, 2 v. 1739

Edwards. 5. 6 180 Taylor, the water poet's motto, Taylor's arrant thief, 1622, Taylor's brief remembrancer of all the Englifh monarchs, 25 heads, 1621

—. 7. _ 181 drunken Barnaby's four journeys, Lat. and Eng. cuts, 1723

—. 3. 6 182 Heydon's (John) glory of the Rofie-crofs—   1664

—. 8. _ 183 Bafil Valentine's laft will and teftament, 1671, and five more

—. 2. _ 184 Wharton's works, by Gadbury   1683

—. 2. 6 185 Bulwer's chirologia, or the natural language of the hand   1644

—. 2. _ 186 Falconer's voyages, Pits's account of the Mahometans

—. 2. 6 187 Milton's hiftory of Great Britain, and 3 more

—. 2. _ 188 œuvres de Racine, 2 t. œuvres de Quevedo, 2 t.

Player —. 1. _ 189 la fcience de la cour, par Limiers 4 t.   Amft. 1723

Chapm.—. 3. 6 190 la fainéte Bible, m g. l. Sedan, 1633, and 2 more

—. 3. _ 191 oeuvres diverfes du Sir D**, Paris, 1743, and 9 more

Macarty—. 3. _ 192 oeuvres de Rabelais, 2 tom, 1691, and 9 more

—. 5. 6 193 l'origin des Puces, 1749, and 4 more

Chapman 7. _ 194 metamorphofis naturalis, authore J. Goedardo, fig. colorat, and 3 more

—. 9. _ 195 novum Teftamentum Græcum, Elz. 1656, and 16 more

(11)

£. s. d
19. 3.

196 H. C. Agrippæ de occult. philofop. Lugduni, and 3 _ ./. _ Man.
 more
197 Dion Caffius, Paris, ap. Rob. Steph. 1544, and 2 more _ ./. _
198 Mather's difcourfe concerning comets, m. g. l. 1683, _. 3. _ Hayes
 ——'s (Cotton) providences relating to witchcraft,
 1691
199 the new Teftament, with annotations, Antwerp 1621, _ .5. 6 WH.
 and 11 more
200 Quarles's hieroglyphikes, 1638, and 9 more — .6. 6. Hayes.
201 Stow's chronicles of England, m. g. l bl. l. 1604, _. 8. 6
 Floddan field, in nine fits — 1664
202 Everardt's fhort hand, 1658, and 3 more, c. t. g. l. — .2. _ Chapm
203 Childrey's natural rarities of England, 1661, and 1 — .2. 6
 more
204 David's fling againft great Goliah, by Hutchins, 1615, — /. 6 Man.
 and 3 more
205 hiftorie of Mary Queen of Scotland, 1636, and 1 more — ./. 6
206 Shakefpeare's poems, m. g. l. 1640, the Pfalms tranf- _. 6. 6 D.r Hunte:
 lated by King James I. m. g. l.
207 the Pfalms, by King James I. morocco back, g. l. _. 2. _ WH.
 and 1 more
208 the hiftory of Gefta Romanorum, bl. l. printed by _ .5. 6 D.r Gifford.
 Bifhop, m. b. Silvefter's parliament of vertues, m. b. _ .5. 6
209 Erafmus's praife of folly, with Holbein's cuts — .5. 6
210 Lord Praiflac's art of war, cuts, m. g. l. Cambridge, _. 7. 6
 printed by R. Daniel 1639
211 Wefley's hiftory of the new Teftament, with Sturt's _. 4. 6 Hayes.
 cuts —— —— 1717
212 the new Teftament in Englifhe, with the tranflation _ .4. _ D.r Gifford
 of Erafmus in Latin, bl. l. Lond. ex officina T.
 Gaultier ——— 1550
213 the ftorm, Nov. 24, 1703, by Defoe, and Glanville of - 3. 6
 witches
214 Addifon's travels, 8vo. fine print 1705 — .5. _
215 Howell's familiar letters, 8vo. — 1754 _. 2. 6
216 Jeffery of Monmouth's Britifh hiftory, by Thompfon, _. 3. 6 Hayes.
 1718
217 life of Dr. Henry More, by Ward, and 3 more — 2. _
218 Budgell's lives and family of the Boyles, 1737, and 3 _ .2. 6
 more
219 Knight's life of Erafmus, cuts, wants the title, half- _ .4. _ Hayes.
 bound, memoirs of Cardinal de Retz, m g. l 1723
220 Neifon's life of Bp. Bull, 1714, and 3 more — .2. _
221 Bounlainvilliers's life of Mahomet, 1731. and 2 more — .5. _
222 ——— . ———'s ancient parliaments of France, 2 v. — .4. 6
 hiftory of France, 2 v. — 1702

£ . s . d
25 . 7 . —

_ . 1 . 6 223 Bennet's memorial of the reformation, 1748, and more

_ . 3 . 6 22 4 Ball's antiquities of Conftantinople, cuts, 1729, Armftrong's hiftory of Minorca —— 1756

_ . 4 . 6 225 Fitzofborne's lettors, 1763, Burnet's account of Switzerland, &c.

_ . 4 . _ 226 Maundrell's journey from Aleppo to Jerufalem, 1697, Pfalmanaazar's defcription of Formofa, cuts, 1704

_ . 6 . _ 227 Buckingham's (Sheffield) works, 2 v. 8vo.   1740

_ 2 . 6 228 Milton's Paradife loft, 8vo. 1678, and 2 more

_ . 4 . 6 229 the dreamer, 1754, Milton's Paradife loft, 8vo. g. l. 1674, and 1 more

_ . 1 . 6 230 Hayward's Britifh mufe, 3 v in 1   1738

_ . 3 . 6 231 Aubrey's mifcellanies, 1721, Glanvill of witches, and 1 more

_ . 1 . _ 232 Confent's ftate of the church of Ruffia, and 3 more

_ . 2 . _ 233 Shere's hiftory of Polybius, 2 v and 1 more

_ . 4 . _ 234 hiftory of Pruffia, 1756, Voltaire's hiftory of Charles XII. of Sweden —— 1732

_ . 2 . 6 235 Fanfhaw's letters, Hill's natural hiftory, and 1 more

Chapman _ . 3 . 6 236 Kirby's Suffolk traveller, 1764, and 1 more

_ . 2 . _ 237 the life of Richard Savage, Earl Rivers, and 2 more

Nichols _ . 3 . 6 238 Anglorum fpeculum, or the worthies of England, in church and ftate —— 1683

Chapm: _ . 4 . _ 239 five pieces of runic poetry, fewed, 1763, and 5 more

_ . 2 . 6 240 Wright's great concern of human life, c. t. g. l. 1733

Hayes _ . 3 . _ 241 Humphrey's account of the propaga ion of the gofpel, c. t. g. l. Goodman's winter evening conference, m. g. l.

_ . 3 . 6 242 Chandler's hiftory of the perfecution, 1736, Lurdner's pieces, m b. —— 1729

_ . 5 . 6 243 Balguy's tracts, with Grove and Bays's anfwers, m. b. ——'s fermons, gilt

_ . 2 . 6 244 fermons by Barker, Newman and Sturmy, 3 v.

_ . 4 . _ 245 —— Maynard, 2 v. — 1737

_ . 3 . 6 246 ——.—— Gale, 4 v. not uniform — 1724

_ . 2 . 6 247 Savage's mifcellaneous poems, l. p. 1726, the medleys for 1711, l. p. — 1712

_ . 5 . 6 248 Waller's poems, l. p. heads —— 1711

_ . 4 . _ 249 memoirs and life of Lord Polingbroke, l. p. 1752, Mallet's life of Lord Bacon, l. p. vellum back, 1740

_ . 1 . 6 250 Proderick's hiftory of the war in the Netherlands, l. p. 1713

£30. _ . _

251 Mead on the plague, 1. p. m. g. l.　　　1729 _ . 2 *52 6 D Gff.*
252 Elstob's English Saxon homily, l. p.　　　170 _ . 2.
253 the voiage and travaile of Sir John Maundeville, l p.' _ . 7. 6 *Payne*
　　　Without Cut.　　　1725
254 historical register, 13 v. bound, and some loose num- _ . 7. _
　　　bers
255 the political state of Great-Britain, from 1711 to 1740, *16.* _ . _ *Payne.*
　　　60 v. complete, 57 bound in red morocco, g. l.
　　　in calf, gilt, and 2 in boards, vol. 60 damag'd

Q U A R T O.

256 Caryl on Job, and 89 more　　　　　　　_ . 1. 6
257 the Apocrypha, m. g. . r. the New Testament, 12mo. _ . 5. _
　　　c. t. g. l. r. printed by Field *badly printed* 1658
258 Carey's poems, Reynolds's view of death, a poem _ . 5. 6
259 Lithgow's travels wants the title, Verstegan's anti- _ . 9. _ *Nichols.*
　　　quities of decayed intelligence　　　Ant. 1605
260 Milton's history of England, heroyk life and death of _ . 3. 6
　　　King Henry the 4th, by Grimstone, 1612, and 1
　　　more
261 Ogilby's Æfop's fables, cuts, Moll's 32 maps of the _ . 3. 6 *Chapman.*
　　　geography of the ancients, coloured　　　1721
262 Frezier's voyage to the South-fea, cuts　　1717 _ . 5. _ *Govr Verelst*
263 Tournefort's voyage into the Levant, 2 v. cuts 1718 _ . 10. 6
264 Hanway's travels over the Cafpian-fea, 4 v. cuts, 1 5. _
　　　best edit.　　——　　　1753
265 Mafcou's history of the ancient Germans, by Lediard, _ . 4. _
　　　2 v. l. p.　　——　　　1738
266 history of the bucaniers of America, cuts, 1695, Lith- _ . 8. _ *Nichols*
　　　gow's 19 years travels, imp.
267 Wefley's poems　　——　　　1736 _ . 4. _
268 the works of Salluft, translated by Gordon　1744 _ . 8. 6 *Govr Verelst*
269 Lenfant's history of the council of Conftance, 2 v. _ . 6. 6
　　　　　　　　　　　　　1730
270 Rolt's life of the Earld of Craufurd, fewed 1753 _ . 1. 6
271 Afhmole's theatrum chemicum Britannicum, c. t. g. l. _ . 9. 6 *Mann.*
　　　1652, Afhmole's way to blifs, m. b. g. l.　1658
272 hiftoria Michaelis Serveti, cum cap. m. b. g. l. Helmf. _ . 8. _
　　　　　　　　　　　　　1528
273 the ancient liturgy of the church of Jerufalem, Greek _ . 4. 6
　　　and Englifh, m. g. l.　——　　　1744
274 the Lord's prayer, in above a hundred languages, g l. _ . 12. 6
　　　　　　　　　　　　　1700

£.s.d
53.15.—

(14)

£. s. d
65. 0. 0

302 Nic, de Lyra in novum Teft.   Venet. 148r — . 3. —
303 Placi lexicon biblicum, nitid. pulch. Colonge. — . 1. _
                                           1536
304 Livii hiftoria Rom. impreffis quentel,   Colon. 1525
305 Tullius de officiis cum comment P. Marfi, nitid. 1496 } — 2. —
306 the poor man's librarie, very fair. m. b. g. l. imp. _ . 6. _ Nicols
   by Daye,   1560
307 legenda aurea, or golden legende emprynted by me 2. 2. _ Dr. Hunter
   Julian Notary   1503
308 Nicolls's hiftory of Thucidides, very fair   1550 — . 11. 6
309 Polycronycon, by Wynkyn de Worde   1527 1495 — . 17. —
310 Fabian's chronicle, m. g. l. imprinted, by John Kings- _ . 15. 6 Hayes
   ton,   1556
311 Halle's chronicle, g. l. printed by Graffton,   1550 — . 17. — Do
312 Gerarde's Herbal, coloured, 2 v. c. t. g. l. 1597 2. 12. _ Nicols.

£ 2. 7

End of the Second Day's Sale.

Third Day's Sale,

SATURDAY, MARCH 30, 1776.

PAMPHLETS.

Nicol _. *11.* - 313 THREE bundles, by Whifton, Woolfton, Middleton and opponents
_. *10.6* 314 two ditto, mifcellaneous, quarto and octavo
_. *2.6* 315 three ditto, religious and controverfy
T. King _. *11.6* 316 two ditto, hiftorical and entertaining
_. *6.* -317 12 fmall bundles for and againft the clergy
_. *3.* _318 four bundles, religious poetry, againft deifts, &c. &c.
-. *9.* _319 fix ditto, popery, trade, &c. &c
Nicol _. *11.* _320 five ditto heraldry, peerage mifcellaneous, &c.
_. *4.6* 321 fix ditto fermons, controverfy, &c. &c.
_. *5.6* 322 five ditto, catechifm, letters, mifcellaneous
Chapm. _. *16.6* 323 two ditto gardening, hufbandry, fifhing, &c.
-. *9.6* 324 one ditto, various fubjects, very curious
_. *5.* _325 three ditto diffenters fermons, and mifcellaneous
_. *13.* _326 fix ditto mifellaneous quarto, &c. fome curious
-. *5.6* 327 one ditto Runne Red Cap, cobler at Gloucefter. &c.
_. *2.* _328 the confpiracy, a tragedy, by Killigrew, 1638, the honeft whore, by Decker, 1635, a king and no king by Beaumont and Fletcher
-. *8.* _329 one bundle from the beginning of George the IIId to the end of Lord Bute's adminiftration

OCTAVO ET DUODECIMO.

B. White _. *8.6* 330 Nobbes's art of trolling, 1612, Markham's arte of fowling, cuts, 1621, and 12 more
_. *3.6* 331 Quillet's calipædia, a poem by Rowe, 1712, Meibomius's ufe of flogging   1718
_. *3.6* 332 Cotton's choice pieces, and 13 more
_. *2.* _333 Bifhop Wilkins of natural religion, and 5 more

£. s. d
7. 11. —

334 Sykes of natural and revealed religion, 1740, and 2 —.4. —
 more
335 Bunyan's pilgrim's progress, 8vo, cuts, 1751, Whif- —. 4. —
 ton's primitive New Testament, c. r.   1745
336 Derham's astro theology, Morgan's physico theoloy —. 2. 6 *Martin*
337 a collection of sermons, tracts, &c. by Hallet, Hud- — 3. 6
 dy, Pierce, &c. 2 y. bound in vellum
338 Holden's sermons, Fawcet's sermons, and 4 more —.2. 6
339 sermons, by Dodwell, Bennet and Dawes, 3 v. —.3. 6
340 ———— Law, Bullock, &c. 4 v. — — — — — —.2. 6
341 ———— Maynard, 2 v. by Scott, 2 v. — 3. 6 *Hayes.*
342 dissenting controversy on the side of liberty, 5 v. m. b. —.6. —
343 Fleming's search after souls, and 3 more — —.2. 6
344 Foster of the christian religion, 1734, and 3 more —. 2. 6
345 the victim, a tragedy, m. g. l, Addison's Cato, m. g. — —.3. 6 *Fox.*
 l. and 3 more
346 Baxter's dying thoughts, m. g. l. and 2 more —. 2. 6
347 Nelson's address to persons of quality, l p. m. g. l, — 3. 6
 and 1 more
348 Sir John Suckling's poems, 1648, m. g. l. and 2 more — 3. — *Chapman*
349 Sturmy's theological theory of a plurality of worlds, — 2. —
 c. t. g. l. and 2 more
350 Biggs's military history of Europe, m. g. l. 1755, — 4. 6
 history of the wars of Cyprus, m. g, l.   1687
351 Watts's miscellaneous thoughts, and 3 more —. 3. 6
352 memoirs of queen Anne, 1729, and 3 more —. 2. —
353 Anglorum speculum, or the worthies of England in —.3. 6
 church and state, 1684, Welwood's memoirs, m,
 b g. history of the Severambians, sewed,   1738
354 Spence's Lucian, Vida's game of chess, and 1 more — 3. —
355 the school of man, 1753, and 1 more — 2. 6
356 mottos to the spectators, tatlers, and guardians, and —. 1. 6
 1 more
357 account of the prosecutions of the quakers, c t. g. l. — 2. — *Fox.*
 and 1 more
358 Jortin of the christian religion, 1746, and 3 more —.2. 6
359 pithy, pleasaunt and profitable works of maister Skel= — 3. —
 ton,   1736
360 the lives and amours of Daphnis and Chloe, cuts —2. 6 *Chapman*
 1746, and 1 more
361 divers parts of scripture, chiefly from Dr. Mills's — 3. —
 Greek Testament, cuts, c. g. l. &c.   1761
362 the life and acts of Syr William Wallace, bl. lett. m. — 3. 6 *Dr. Hunter*
 b. g.   Edinb 1620
363 Mundy's chronicle from the creation, bl. lett. m. b. g. — 3. —

1611

-. 2. - 364 a cat may look upon a king, 1714, Daniel Defoe's
    jure divino, with his head

-. 3. 6 365 the court regifter and ftatefman's remembrancer, and
    5 more

Fox. -. 9. 6 366 fpaccio della beftia trionfante, or the expulfion of
    the triumphant beaft, by Giordano Bruno, by To-
    land, very fcarce

F. -. 6. 6 367 Novum Teftamentum Gr. Curcéllæi, Amft. 1711,
    and 5 more

D⁰Hunter. - 10. - 368 hiftoriale defcription de l'Ethiopie, Anvers, 1558,
    and 7 more

Crookfhanks 2. - 369 imagines mortis, ad hæc medicinæ animæ, cum fig.
    Coloniæ, 1567, la metamorphofe d'Ovide, figure,
    à Lyon, 1513

-. 1. 6 370 Polydori Vergilii hiftoriæ Anglicæ, 2 v. Gandavi,
    1556

-. 1. 371 Theophrafti hiftoria plantarum, per Gaza, Par. 1529

-. 1. -372 chronicorum libellus, Frankfort, 1542

-. 2. 6 373 Moriæ encomium, ftulticiæ laudatio, Frobenii, m. b.
    Bafil, 1,51, Chriftus triumphans comœdia apoca-
    lyptica, a J. Foxo, m g. l. Bafil, per Oporium, 1556

-. 2. 6 374 ad inclytos ac præpotentes Angliæ proceres ordines
    et ftatus, &c. authore Jo Foxo, m. g. l. Bafil, per
    Oporium, 1559

D⁰Hunter -. 1. 6 375 Flores Avicenne, m. g. l. Lyons, 1514

M⁰carly -. 2. 6 376 acta Romanorum pontificum, Balei, m. g l. Baf.
    1558

-. 1. 6 377 Cajetani opera tentacula Nov. Teft. m. g. l. Lyon,
    1529

-. 2. 6 378 Biblia facra, Thielman Kerver, m. g. l. Par. 1634

-. 3. - 379 hiftorie Palladienne, traitant des geftes et d'ameurs,
    &c. m. g. l. Par. 1573

-. 7. 6 380 Torbuck's parliamentary debates, 9 v. 1741

-. 4. 6 381 quadriennium annæ poftremum ; or the political ftate
    of Great Britain, 8 v. in 4, half bound 1718

-. 4. 6 382 the fame book, 6 v. in 3, gilt, borders of gold, &c.

Cater 4 8. - 383 the political ftate of Great-Britain, 58 v. half bound,
    4 v. a little imperfect

D⁰Harwood 1. 8. 384 a collection of fermons and tracts, by eminent diffent-
    ers, 30 v. uniformly half bound and lettered

QUARTO.

- 12. - 385 Brown's travels, cuts, m. b. g. l. cuts, 1673, Ran-
   ... dolph's ftate of the Morea, cuts, 1686

£. s. d
21. 15. –

386 Sir Francis Drake's voyages, with his portrait, m. — .*3.* –
  g. l   1653
387 James's ftrange and dangerous voyage, m g. l.   — .*6.* –
388 Hayward's life and reign of Edward the VIth, with — .*3. 6*
  their portraits. m. b. g. l.   1630
389 Coverte's voyage and travels, bl. lett. m. b. 1612, — .*6. 6* *Nicol.*
  an account of Monf. de Quefne's late expedition at
  Chio, *Bds.*   1683
390 Daniel's civil wars between the houfes of Lancafter — .*4.* –
  and York, m. b. l.   1609
391 the life of Robert Bruce king of Scots, a poem, neat, — .*2.* – *Fox.*
                               1729
392 an account of the bucaniers of America, cuts, 1684, — .*7.* –
  a volume of voyages and travels, for December,   .
  1708, cuts
393 Defaguliers's fyftem of experimental philofophy, cuts, — .*4.* –
  m. g. l. 1719, Sprat's hiftory of the royal fociety,
                               1728
394 the pleafant hiftory of Parifmus prince of Bohemia, — .*5. 6*
                               1704
395 Carleton's thankful remembrance of God's mercy, — .*4.* – *B. White*
  cuts, m. b. g. l. *E. Bollifant.*   1627
396 Warner's Albion's England, m. g. l. a fine copy, 1602 — .*6. 6*
397 Clarke's lives of eminent divines, cuts,   1654 — .*5.* –
398 Grimftone's heroic life and deplorable death of Henry — *1. 6*
  the IVth,   1612
399 Keith's hiftory of Virginia pt. 1ft, m. b. 1738, and — .*2. 6*
  2 more
400 Ogilby's roads of England, Petty's 32 maps of Ire- — *4.* –
  land, and 1 more
401 Fletcher's purple ifland, pifcatoire eclogs, &c. 1633 — .*5.* –
402 Ward's England's reformation, a poem, Guarini's — .*3. 6*
  paftor fido,   1618
403 Barkley's Argenis, or the loves of Polyarchus and — *2. 6* *Fox.*
  Argenis, by Long, 1636, and 3 more
404 Urchard's epigrams divine and moral, m. b. 1646, — .*4.* – *Nicol*
  Harrington's epigrams, pleafant and ferious, m. b.
  g. l.   1615
405 Taylor's water cormorant, his complaint againft a — .*1. 6* *Fox*
  brood of land cormorants, in 14 fatyrs
406 Anton's vice's anatomie, fcourged and corrected, in — .*2.* – *Nicol*
  new fatyrs, m. b g. l.   1617
407 the negociations of Cardinal Wolfey, m. b g. l. 1641, — .*5.* – *Chapman*
  and 4 more

£. s. d

26. 8. —

£. s. d
31. 11. –

429 more ftrange newes of flouds in England, no date — . 1. 6
430 Lylie's Eupheus, the anatomie of wit, m. b. g. 1636 — . 4. –
431 Peterfon's greatnefs of cities, 1606, The bellman of — . 3. 6 *Thane*
London, bringing to light the moft notorious villa-
nies, 1616, &c. &c.
432 the inftruction of a chriften woman, printed by Wykes — . 6. — *Dr Gifford*
1523
433 Higgin's mirrour for the magiftrates, Ruffia back — . 9. 6
1578
434 the Ethiopian hiftory of Heliodorus, by Underdown, — . 11. 6 *Nicol*.
m. g. l. 1606
435 amorum Troili & Crefeida, or the loves of Troilus & — . 6. — *Do*
Creffida, Lat. and Eng m. g l. 1638
436 Ciceronis amor, Tullies love, by greene, bound in — . 6. — *Do*
green, 1628
437 the inftitution of a chriften man, m. g. l. by Berthelet, — . 8. —
1537
438 the hiftorie of two the mofte noble captaines of the — . 6. 6 *Do*
worlde, Anniball and Scipio, m. g. l. by Berthelet,
1544
439 an auncient hiftorie and exquifite chronicle of the — . 12. 6
Romanes warres both civile and foren, by Appian
m g. l. imprinted by Raufe Newberry 1578
440 the dialogues of the creatures moraly fed, right profi- 2. 12. 6 *Dr Chaun.*
table to the governaunce of man, with curious *cey*.
wooden cuts, m. g. l. N. B. See the manufcript
before the title. (*Suppofed to be tranflated & printed by
John Raftall,*)
FOLIO.

441 the rogue, or the life of Gufman de Alfarache and 5 — . 6. 6 *Vanden*
more
442 Dr. Sacheverel's trial, m. g. l. and 1 more — . 5. –
443 Hobbes's laviathan, m. g. l. 1651, Howard and Or- — . 7. – *F.*
rery's plays, m. g. l. 1668
444 Blackmore's Eliza, an epick poem, m. g. l. r. 1705, — . 5. –
Beaumont's Pfyche, or love's myftery, 1702
445 Brown's travels, cuts, 1685, Olearius's travels of the — . 8. 6 *Fox*
ambaffadors, 1662
446 Speed's hiftory of Great-Britain 1632 — . 14. 6 *Jones*
447 Stow's furvey of London, a fair copy 1633 — . 3. –
448 More's theological works and 2 more *bds* — . 2. 6
449 Kennet's hiftorical regifter and chronicle, 1744, — . 16. 6 *Macarty*
Nicolfon's Englifh hiftorical library 1714

£. s. d
41. 7 -

—. *6.* - 450 Burchet's naval hiſtory of England 1720
Young —. *6.* -- 451 Stafford's pacata Hibernia, 1633, Hume's hiſtory of
Scotland
Thane —. *5. 6* 452 Murray's laws and acts of parliament of Scotland,
Edin. 1681
Chaſmⁿ —. *5. 6* 453 Fuller's church hiſtory of England, with the hiſt. of
Cambridge, 1656
—. *6. 6* 454 Anderſon's royal genealogies of emperors kings, &c.
1736
—. *4.* —455 Oldmixon hiſtory of the houſe of Stuart, 1730, Sam-
mes's antiquities of ancient Britain, 1676
—. *4.* —456 Archerley's Britanic conſtitution, 1727, Burnet's memoirs of the dukes of Hamilton, 1677
—. *3.* — 457 the Athenian mercury, compleat, 1691, the old whig,
or conſiſtent proteſtant 1734
—. *9. 6* 458 Bp. Burnet's hiſtory of his own times, 2 v. 1724
—. *3.* —459 the votes, for 1747 and 48, and 4 more
—. *2.* —460 Ibraham or the illuſtrious Baſſa, by Scudery and 2
more
Williams —. *7. 6* 461 Yorke's union of honour, with his portrait, 1640,
Brooke's catalogue of honour 1619
Graves —. *3.* — 462 Du Bartas's divine works, g. l, 1633, Whateley on
the book of Geneſis, with his portrait, 1640
—. *3.* —463 Jameſon on the pentateuch half bound, 1748
Jones —. *6. 6* 464 Burnet's theory of the earth, 2 v. 1697, ſtate letters,
in Oliver Cromwell's time, ſewed 1743
Dr Hun. —. *18. 6* 465 voyage de ſa Majeſte Britannique in Hollande, avec
-ter. fig. 1692
Cater - —. *7.* —466 Parker de anquitate Britanicæ eccleſiæ, fig. per Drake
1729
Connant —. *11.* —467 Reading catalogus bibliothecæ collegio Sionenſi,
1724, catalogus librorum manuſcrip. bibliothecæ
Cottonianæ *With Head* 1696
P —. *2. 6* 468 Hyde catalogus bibliothecæ Bodleianæ Oxon. 1674
P —. *6.* —469 catalogus librorum MSS. Angliæ & Hiberniæ, Oxon
1697
P —. *6.* —470 Rowe's Lucan's Pharſalia, l. p. 1718
3. 6. —471 Harris's collection of voyages and travels, 2 v. cuts,
beſt edition, a fine copy 1744
1. 3. — 472 Holinſhed's chronicles, 2 v. in one, very fair 1580
Shropſhire *1. 14.* —473 the worckes of Thomas Becon, 3 v. a fine copy, with
the portraits, of the author and Printer, c. t. g l.
borders of gold, imprinted, by Daye 1564

End of the Third Day's Sale.

£53 (16.6)

*2ⁿᵈ vol. imperfect.

Fourth Day's Sale,

SATURDAY, MARCH 30, 1776.

Pamphlets.

474 FIFTY sermons, &c. gilt leaves   — . 2 . 6
475 one large bundle of sermons and tracts, 1640 to — . 3 . —
     to the restoration   *Chapman*
476 two bundles, miscellaneous, sermons, tracts, &c. some — . 5 . — *Roger*
     very curious
477 two ditto, miscellaneous   —   —   —   *Dr Harwood.* . 7 . 6
478 three large bundles, of George I. and II. — — — — . 17 . — *Nicol.*
479 six bundles, controversy, miscellaneous, &c. _ . _ _ — . 18 . — *Harwood*
480 three ditto, natural philosophy, education, and un- _ . 18 . 6
     common subjects   *Barclay.*   s
481 four ditto, against popery, baptism, &c. . . . . . — . 4 . —
482 five ditto, historical, martial, peerage, East-India af- 1 . 9 . — *Collins*
     fairs, &c.
483 five ditto, miscellaneous, divinity   — . 5 . — *Do*
484 five ditto, folio, quarto &c. various   — . 4 . — *Do*
485 Wanley's wonders of the little world, 4to. in numbers, — . 7 . — *Cater*
     complete
486 31, very curious, on witchcraft. and astrology, with — . 9 . *Pennant*
     uncommon cuts

OCTAVO & DUODECIMO,

487 Middleton's cookery and 10 more on cookery and — . 4 . — *Collins.*
     physic
488 theatre de Corneile, &c   — . 2 . 6

£.s.d
6.6. -

Elmsley -. 8.6 489 Du Lude's treatife of fpirits, 1723, and 9 more, on witchcraft, &c.

-. 6.6 490 an addition declatorie to the bulles, with a fearching of the maze, imprinted at London, by John Daye, *D*. £1.1. - W*. and 26 more, fmall, bl. l.

-. 3. - 491 whimzies, or a new caft of characters, 1631, and 9 more

-. 2.6 *491 Bifhop Burnet's paftoral cure, and 11 more

-. 3. - 492 the court of curiofity, dreams and vifions, 1681, and 2 more

Graves -. 5. - 493 Herrick's Hefperides, human and divine, 1648, and and 9 more

-. 2.6 494 Bott's anfwer to Warburton's divine legation, and 19 more

Nicol -. 7.6 495 Heywood's hiftory of women, 1657, Bulwer's artificial changl ng, with his portrait, 1650, and 2 more

Collins-. 4.6 496 oeuvres de St. Evremond, tom. 1ft, 3d and 4th, and 17 more

-. 4.- 497 Lilium medicinæ, a mfs. on vellum, and 1 more mfs.

-. 4.- 498 almanacks, 1754, &c. 2 v. and 7 more, m. g. l. and 7 more

-. 3.6 499 Dryden's mifcellanies, fin. edit. 1716, v. 1ft and 2d, in 1 v. m. g. l. and 2 more

-. 3.6 500 Plutarch's morals, 3 odd v. m. g. l. and 2 more

-. 4.- 501 Shuckford's facred hiftory, v. 1ft, and 8 more

-. 3. - 502 Marfhall's fermons, v. 3d, and 9 more

-. 6.- 503 Morgan's moral philofopher, 3 v. Jurieu's critical hiftory, 2 v.

-. 2. - 504 Horneck's fermons, 2 v, 1698, and 4 more

-. 3.6 505 Burrow's effay on divine providence, 1725, and 4 more

-. 3. - 506 Norris's treatife of humility, and 4 more

Nicol -. 4. - 507 Toland's letters to Serena, 1704, Lord Herbert's ancient religion of the Gentiles, by Lewis 1711

Dr.Giff d. 2.6 508 magna charta, cum ftatutis Ant. printed by Tottiil, 1587, and 5 more

W. -.6.6 509 Goughe's original of the Turkifh empyre, with the horrible acte of Solton Soliman, bl. l, imprinted by Thomas Marfhe, a compendious and moft marveylous hiftory of the latter times of the Jewes, b. l. 1561, and 3 more

Hayes.-.4.6 516 merry jefts, concerning popes, monkes and friers, bl. l. printed by Eld, 1617, and 8 more

-. 4.6 511 Swift's tale of a tub, 8vo. cuts Blackmore on the creation, and 1 more

£. s. d
11. 7. 6

512 Dryden and Swift's miscellany poems, 7 odd vol. — 5. –
513 Carter's analysis of honor and armory, 1655, and 3 — 2. 6
more
514 the voyages and adventures of Miles Philips, 1724, — 2. –
and 1 more
515 Gordon's geographical grammar, Echard's gazetteer — 4. 6
516 a collection of puritan tracts, by Nichols, Wheten- — 12. — *Hayes*
hall, &c. 9 v. finely bound in red Morocco, very
scarce
517 fugitive pieces in profe and verse, publiſhed by Mr. 1. 19. — *Nicol*.
Walpole, m. g. l.   Strawbery-hill, 1758
*517 Hentzer's journey into England, Lat. and Eng. by 1. 13. –
Mr. Walpole, neat,   Strawberry-hill, 1757
518 Brown's hymns. c. t. g. l. and 4 more   — 2. –
519 catalogus bibliothecæ Harleianæ, 5 v,   1743 — 6. –
520 imperial magazine for 1760, 61 and 62, 3 v.   — 3. 6 *Martin*
521 univerfal magazine, 11 v.   1747 — 11. 6
522 fable of the bees, 8vo. Thompfon's feafons, 8vo. — 5. 6
523 Coſtard's letters to Martin Folkes, Efq; concerning — 7. — *Nicol*
the rife and progreſs of aſtronomy amongſt the
ancients, 2 y. m. l, g.   1746
524 Cockburn's hiſtory of duels, 1 p. m. g. l. 1720, an — 4. —
impartial vindication of the Eaſt-India company,
m. g. l.
525 Littleton's tenures, imprinted at Lond. by Tottell, — 2. 6 *WH*.
1581, and 5 more
526 Seneca's morals, 8vo. 1678, and 6 more   — 4. — *Collins*
527 Geddes's mifcellaneous tracts, and 9 more   — 5. —
528 the tatler, v. 1ft and 2d. l. p.   1710 — 3. 6
529 Carter's Epictetus, Dubl. 1759, Rofcommon's poems — 6. 6
1717
530 Lardner's credibility of the gofpel hiſtory, 7 odd v. — 3. — *Roby*.
531 a collection of mifcellaneous tracts, 11 v.   — 5. –
532 ————— ———— fermons, in alphabetical order, 34 v. 1. 6. —
boards
533 the political ſtate of Great-Britain, 58 v. in 53, bound, 4. —. —
half bound, &c. the year 1731 imperfect
534 horologium orat. greco fpectans ad facerdotes, m. g. l. —. 5. 6
1509, horæ beatis virginis, m. g. l. G. Colon. 1517
535 Statii opera, m. g. l. Bafill. 1541, de reformatione — 3. 6
virium anime,   1493

D

£. s. d
25. 9. 6　　　　　　(26)

Wodhull. _. 4. - 536 vita Chrifti fecundum Bonaventuram, m. g. l. Paris,
　　　　　　pfalterium facrarum literarum carminæ et preca-
　　　　　　tiones, per Caftalione, m. g. l.　　　　Bas. 1547
Hayes. - 3. - 537 concordata inter Leonem X. pont. max. opera, M.
　　　　　　Cofmæ Guymier, m. g. l. Par. 1550, exempla
　　　　　　facre fcripture, per Regnault Chandiere, m. g. l.
　　　　　　Paris
Fox. - 3. - 538 defenforum et declaratio privilegionum fratrum men-
　　　　　　dicatum, m. g. l. 1508, Gerfon compendium theo-
　　　　　　logie de facramento baptifmi, m. g. l. Par. 1508
Dr Gifford 3. 6 539 Ifiodorus de fummo bono, m. g. l. per Jean Petit,
　　　　　　1502, fermones declamati coram alma univers.
　　　　　　Cantibrigienfi, m. g. l.
_. 2. 6 540 fermones Jacobi de Voragine, m. g. l. per Petit, Par.
　　　　　　1503, regula canonicorum regularium, m. g. l.
_. 2. 6 541 fummula Ramundi fept. facrament. m. g. l. Paris,
　　　　　　apud Thileman Kerver, 1516
_. 2. - 542 D'Orbellus fuper 4 libri fententiarum, m. g. l.
　　　　　　Lugd. 1503
Macarty _. 7. - 543 catalogus hereticorum, m. g. l. 1526, modus eligendi
　　　　　　ac poftulandi prelatos, m. g. l.　　　　1509
Dr Hunter _. 2. _ 544 opera varia Symphorioni Champerii, m g. l.
_. 2. _ 545 fcholaftica hiftoria magiftri Petri Comeftoris, m. g. l.
　　　　　　Lugd. 1526
_. 1. 6 546 fermones de fanctis, M. g. l. Lugd. per Ant. du Ry.
　　　　　　1523
Fox. _. 3. 6 547 le Noveau Teftament, par Calvin, m. g. l.　1551

Q U A R T O.

_. 2. 6 548 Gregory's works, 1684, and 5 more
_. 2. 6 549 Patrick's parable of a pilgrim and 5 more
_. 3. _ 550 Selden's hiftory of tithes and 7 more
Hayes _. 3. _ 551 Goodwin's catalogue of Englifh bifhops, bl. l. 1615,
　　　　　　and 3 more
Mole _. 8. 6 552 Foxe's fermon at Paul's crofs, bl. l. Lond. imprinted
　　　　　　by Daye, 1570, and 2 more
Dodd. _. 3 6 553 Stow's defcription of England, &c. bl. l: wants the
　　　　　　title,　　　　　　1600
_ 1. 6 554 common places of the chriftian religion, by Man, bl.
　　　　　　l. printed by Pennyman, 1578, a treatife of hea-
　　　　　　venly philofophy, bl. l. Lond. imprinted by Nor-
　　　　　　ton,　　　　　　1578
Hayes. _. 5. _ 555 Lowman on the revelation of St. John,　　1737

20.15.6

556 Cumberland's laws of nature, by Maxwell, l. p. 1772 - 3.6
557 Norden's defcription of Cornwall, cuts,   1728 - 6._
558 Dale's hiftory and antiquities of Harwich and Dover - 10.6
    court, l. p. cuts,   1730
559 Powel's hiftory of Wales, wants the title, bl. l. m. - 8.6 Young
    b. g. l.   1584
560 hiftory of Europe, 6 v. monthly chronicle, 3 v.   - 6._
561 Macauley's hiftory of England, v. 2d. 1765, the Har- _ 5. _
    leian mifcellany, v. 1ft,   1744
562 Blainvill's travels. v. 1ft, and 3 more   _ 5; _ Mann
563 hiftoire generale des voyages, avec fig. tom. 4, 7, 8 - 6. _
    et 9 ——— Haye 1747
564 Spenfer's faerie queene, 2 v. a fair copy   1595 _ 14.6 Horne.
565 ———'s poems of the world's vanitie, a fair copy, _ 7. _
                                             1591
566 Whitney's choice emblemes, bound in green morocco, 1.2. _ Nicol.
                                             1586
567 the life of Mahomet, the conqueft of Spain, and the _ 2.6
    ruin of the Sarazen empire, taken from a mfs. copy,
    faid to be wrote by Sir Walter Rawleigh
568 Stukely's account of Richard of Cirencefter, 1757, - 6. _ B. White.
    parlæographia Britannica, part 2d and 3d   1746
569 three Stukley's medallic hiftory of Caraufius, emperour - 10.6
    of Britain, part 2d, cuts, in fheets   1759
570 Fairfax's declaration of the engagements, remon- - 11.6 D. Hunter
    ftrances, &c. 1647, and 2 more
571 Greene's poet's vifion and a prince's glorie, 1603, _ 12.6 Nicol.
    Drayton's poem, 1603, and 1 more
572 a Saxon hiftorie, of the admirable adventures of Clo- _ 8. 6 D.
    doaldus and his three children, 1634, Lord's difco-
    verie of the feft of the Banians   1630
573 Warner's Albion's England, m. b. g. l.   1602 _ 6.6
574 hiftory of tbe feven champions of Chriftendom, b. l. _ 7. _
    1626, and 3 more
575 Lylie's Euphues, the anatomy of wit, b. l. fair, 1579, _ 5 6 Mafon
    Cleland's inftitution of a young nobleman, 1607,
    Lodge's Euphues' golden legacy   1634
576 Seneca's tragedis, by Heywood, bl. l. fair, wants the - 6.6 Nicol.
    title, imprinted by Marks   1581
577 the thrie tailes of the thrie priefts of Peblis, bl. l. im- 1.10. _ Gough.
    printed at Edinb. be Robert Charteris   1603
578 regimen fanitatis Salerni, Paris, par Petit, m. g. l. _ 3.6
                                              1505

£. s. d

39. —. 6

Nicol —. 8. — 579 Greene's never too late, fent to young gentlemen,
——— ghoft haunting cony-catchers, 1626, Greene's
groat's worth of wit, bought with a million of re-
,pentance ——— 1637

Hayes. —. 2. 6 580 Thomas's principal rules of the Italian grammer. bl.
l. Lond imprinted by by Berthelet, 1550. a poaft
with a pacquet of letters, bl. l Lond printed by
Fabian ——— 1685

—. 2. —.581 Blower's ftore houfe or treafurie for the deceafed, bl.
l. 1631, Hill's arte of gardening, part 1ft, bl. l.
Lond imprinted by Alde 1608

—. 3. — .582 hiftory of Palmerin, prince of England, part 1ft, bl. l.
by Munday, 1639. Greene's pleafant hiftory of Dò-
raftus and Fawnia, bl. l. ——— 1629

—. 3. — 583 a Latin manufcript on vellum

Fox —. 3. — 584 Luther on the Galatians, bl. l. 1603, and 6 more

Thane. —. 6 — 585 the year-book, bl. l. m. b. g. l. printed by Pynfon,
1521

Fox —. 7. — 586 hiftoire de l'origine de l'imprimerie, Haye, 1740, and
3 more

Thane —. 8. — 587 Icones & hiftoriæ regum Francorum, Franc. 1622, and
3 more

D°. —. 1. 6 588 Vegetius de re militari, 1607, and 3 more

—. 6. — 589 Bate s jewel-houfe of art and nature, and 3 more

—. 4. — 590 Goodwin's being filled with the fpirit, with his portrait, and 4 more

—. 5. 6 591 the Æneis of Virgil, tranflated by Trapp, 2 v, boards
1713

—. 8. — 592 Buckingham's (Sheffield) works, 2 v. 1723

F. 3. 10. — 593 incipit liber qui vocatur fpeculum chriftiani, m. g. l.
printed by Macklinia

D?Hunter —. 16. — 594 the fruytfull faynges of Davyde the kynge in the feven
penytencyal pfalmes, c. r. very fair, printed by
Pynfon ——— 1505

Hayes —. 18. 6 595 Batman's doome, warning all men to the judgmente.
ftraunge prodigies, &c. c. r. with wood cuts, Lond.
imprinted, by Ralph Nubery 1581

D?Hunter 1. 3. — 596 here begynneth a devout treatyfe in Englyfhe, called
the pylgrimage of perfectione, for all chriften peo-
ple to rede, m. g. l. imprinted by Richard Pynfon

Mole. —. 13. 6 597 the booke intytuled the floure of the commaundements
of God with many examples prouffytable to all peo-
ple, m. g. l. impr. at Lond. by Wynkyn de Worde,
1510

£. s. d
49. 1. —

598 the new teſtament of king Edward VI. with wood cuts, — .10. 6 Nicol
and 3 portraits of king Edward, neat, Lond. impr.
by Rycharde Jugge 1552
599 catalogus fanctorum, m. g. l. Ludg. impreſſ. Lyons, — .4. —
1509
600 breviarum fecundum, ad uſum Sarum, in memb. m. 2. 2. _Macarty
g. l. in Henry 7th's reign, by Pynfon

F O L I O.

601 Burnet's hiſtory of the reformation, v. 1ſt, Purchas's — .7. 6 Vandenberg
pilgrimage, v. 2d.
602 Biblia facra, Junii et Tremellii, and 1 more — .3. —
603 Dugdale monaſticon Anglicanum, v. 1ſt, cum fig. — 11. 6 Thane
1655
604 Churchill's collection of voyages and travels, v. 3d, — 5. 6 White
half-bound ——— — 1755
605 Pococke's travels, a deſcription of the Eaſt, v. 1ſt, cuts — 10. — Nicol
1733
606 Wither's collection of emblemes, with his portrait, — 12. _ Do
1635
607 Heywood's hierarchie of angells, cuts, 1649, Hey- — .4. _ Collins
wood's hiſtory of women
608 Guicciardini's hiſtory of the warres of Italie, by Fen- — ; 3 _Vanden18
ton 618, and 5 more
609 Machiavell's works, 1680, Edmunds's Cæfar's com- — .8. 6
ment. m. g. l. 1655
610 Stillingfleet's origines facræ, 1702, and 2 more — .3. _Fox.
611 St. Cyprian s works, by Marſhall, 1727, Baxter's ca- — .3. _
tholic theology
612 Knowles's hiſtory of the Turks, 1610, and 2 more — .3. _Fox.
613 Milton s Paradiſe loſt, cuts, 1688, Cowley's works, — .5. _
1672
614 Fuller's holy war and holy ſtate, 2 v. in one, with — 5. —
heads, 1647, Clarke's looking glaſs for faints and
finners, with his portrait 1671
615 Broughton's works 1662, and 3 more — .3. _Fox
616 Evelyn of foreſt trees, m. g. l. Rea's Flora 1676 — .3. _Do Hunt
Mann 617 Scott's difcovery of witchcraft, 1665, and 3 more — .6. 6
Thane 618 Yorke's union of honour, with his portrait 1640 — 5. _
Do 619 Bayle's general dictionary, vol. 1, 2, 3, 6 and part of — 19. 0
the 7th
Fox. 620 Mrs. Philips's poems, m. g. l. Drayton's poems, with — .6. 6
his head, aud 1 more

Fox. —. 3. — 621 Sandy's travels, cuts, 1637, Gage's furvey of the
Weft-Indies ———— 1655

—. 3.6 622 Prynne's life of King John — 1670

—. 4. 6 623 Elton's compleat body of the art military, c. t. g. l.
1650, and 6 more

—. 4.6 624 King James's works, 1616, with the portrait of
Charles I, and 4 more

—. 5.6 625 Charnock's works, vol. 1ft, Motraye's travels, vol. 3d

—. 8. — 626 univerfal hiftory, ancient part, vol. 1ft and 2d, 1736

—. 12. — 627 Chambers's dictionary, vol. 1ft, half-bound, uncut,
feventh edition ——— 1751

—. 4. — 628 the freeholder's journal, the old whig, Pafquin, by
Amherft, &c. and 5 more

Vandenfs—. 4. — 629 Roberts's merchant's map of commerce, 1638, with
his portrait, by Glover

—. 4 — 630 a volume containing 98 prints coloured

Nicol. 2.4. — 631 Recorde's caftle of knowledge, cuts, 1556, Cunning-
ham's cofmographical glafs, cuts, with his portrait,
very fcarce, printed by Daye 1559

—. 10.6 632 Collins's Great-Britain's coafting pilot 1756

—. 18. — 633 Pitt's large Englifh Atlas, 4 v. Oxford 1680

Thane. 1. 0. — 634 Barclay's ftultifera navis, the fhype of fooles, bl. l. a
fair copy ——— 1570

Dr. Giff.d —. 6. — 635 Chaucer's workes, bl. l. imprinted at London, by
Wyllyam Bonham

Nicol. 1.7. — 636 Bochas's fall of princes and other nobles, tranflated
into Englyfhe, by John Ludgate, monke of Bury,
bl. l. cuts, a fair copy, imprinted by Pynfon, 1527

B. White 5.7.6 637 the ftorye of the moft noble and worthy Kynge Arthur and valyaunt knyghtes of the round table, a
fair copy, finely bound, London, imprinted by
Thomas Eaft

1. 8. — 638 the vertuofe boke of diftyllacyon of the waters of all
maner of herbes, with the figures, a fair copy, m.
g. l. imprinted by Andrewe

2.15. — 639 the myrror of the worlde, or thymage of the fame, bl.
l. wants one leaf, printed by Caxton 1480

Mole 3. 13. 6 640 the whole workes of W. Tyndall, J. Frith and Dr.
Barnes, a fine copy, m. g. l. London, printed by
John Daye 1572

Mason. 2. 8. — 641 Fabyan's cronycle, a faircopy, c. t. g. l. bl. l. prented
at London, by Wyllyam Raftell 1533

—. 18.6 642 the holy Bible, b. l. c. r. imprinted at London, by
Barker ——— 1634

End of the Fourth Day's Sale.

£ 84.2.0

Fifth Day's Sale,

MONDAY, APRIL 1, 1776.

PAMPHLETS.

643 SIX bundles, by Sherlock, Hoadly, Chubb, and . . 0. –
    opponents
644 four ditto, miscellaneous, political, South-Sea, &c. 1.12._Chapman
645 three ditto, lives, memoirs, &c.   – .16._Do
646 four ditto, grammars, arts and sciences,'&c.   – .9. – Nicol
647 three ditto, dissenters sermons, &c.   – .8. –
648 three ditto, tithe bill, quakers, trials, &c.   – .9. –
649 three ditto, diverting, entertaining and uncommon 1. 1. –
650 two, Stukeley's account of Richard of Cirencester, _.4._ Mole
    sheets   —   1757

OCTAVO & DUODECIMO.

651 Life and actions of Oliver Cromwell, 1660, and 15 _.5. –
    more lives
652 Bunyan's holy war, and 10 more   _.3. –
653 Fenner's soul's looking glasse, with his portrait, 1640, _.2. –
    and 3 more
654 Flexman, &c. psalms and hymns, m. g. l. 1770, and ·3. –
    three more
655 Sherlock on death, 1691, and twelve more   – .5. –
656 Bishop Hoadley's answer to Sherlock, &c. 3 v. l. p. – .3. –
    and two more
657 Cumberland's Sanchoniatho's Phenician history, 1720, – .5._ Mole
    Mandeville's fable of the bees, vol. first, 1725, and
    one more
658 Quarle's Argalus and Parthenia, cuts, Young's love – 2.6 Collins
    of fame, and three more
659 Grillet's voyages to South America, 1698, Frogers _3.6 Nicol.
    voyage, cuts, and one more

£. s. d
6. 18. -

-. 3. - 660 Quincy's difpenfatory, 1733, Radcliffe's ditto 1721
-. 5. - 661 chemiftry, painting, architecture, &c, tar-water pro
and con, Morgan's practice of phyfic, and one more
Chapman. -. 5. 6 662 Somner's treatife of the Roman ports and forts in Kent,
1693, Addifon's revolutions of Fez and Morocco,
1671, ard three more
Nicol. -. 8. - 663 Withers's crums and fcraps found in a prifoner's bas-
ket in Newgate, 1661, ———— abufes ftript and
whipt, 1615, the legend of Captain Jones, 1656,
and three more
Chapman -. 2. 6 664 Phillips's Maronides, or Virgil traverfty, 1673, and
five more
D°. -. 4. - 665 emblemes of love in four languages, cuts, 1683, and
five more
-. 4. 6 666 the pleafant adventures of Lazarillo de Tormes, 1688,
and eleven more
-. 2. 6. 667 Pettus's conftitution of parliaments in England, 1680,
and eleven more
D° -. 5. 6 668 Olai Magni Gothi de ritu gentium & nat. rerum, cum
fig. and fifteen more
-. 5. - 669 Commenius's gate to the Latin tongue unlocked, 1656,
with his portrait by Crofs, Hoole's orbis pictus,
cuts, and fix more
-. 2. 6. 670 the works of Sir David Lindefey, Knt, b. l. 1670,
and feven more
Mole -. 4. - 671 liber Pfalmorum. Græce, m, g, l, Antv. ap. Graph.
1533, Novum Teftamentom, m, g, l, Antv. ap.
Plantin 1564
Dr. Hunter -. 1. 6 672 Iamblicus de myfteriis Ægyptiorum, &c, m, g, l,
Lug. ap. Tornefium, 1549, harmoniæ evangelicæ,
lib, 4, authore Ofiandro, Lutet. ap. Rob. Step. 1545
-. 2. - 673 Dionyfii Halicarnaffei antiquitat. m, g, l, Lug. ap.
Frellonium ———— 1563
Martin -. 3. - 674 Jofephi antiq, Judaicarum, 2 v, m, g, l, Ludg. ap.
Vincentium ———— 1557
-. 3. - 675 Biblia facra, m. g, l, Antv. ex off. Plantini 1565
Cater -. 6. - 676 Alciati emblemata, cum fig, m, g, l, Ludg. ap. Ro-
vilium ———— ———— 1553
White -. 2. 6 677 a godly and wholfome prefervative againft difpera-
cion at al times neceffarye for the foul, b, l, imp,
at London, by Copland, 1551, and three more
Rogers -. 3. 6 678 the Chriften ftate of matrymonye, b, l, by Miles Coverdale, imp, at London by Hyll, 1552, and 3 more
W. -. 6. 6 679 a godlye newe ftory of twelve men that Moyfes fent
to fpye out the land of Canaan, b, l, imp, at Lond,
by Hill, 1548, and one more

£.
0. 17. 6

680 the boke of the olde God and the newe, of the olde _ .'2. _
   faith and the newe, or the orygynal begynnynge of
   idolatrye, b. l. wants title, Lond. imp. by Byddell,
   and one more

681 a proclamacyon of the hygh empereur Jefu Chrift, b. l. _ .3. _ *Rogers*
   m. g. l. Lond. imp by Redman, the abominable
   blafphemies contain'd in the maffe, b. l. m. g. l.
   Lond. im by Powell   —   1548

682 the old fayth of Greate Brittaygne, b. l. m. g. l. and _.3. _ *Tutet*
   2 more curious tracts, no date, a godly invective in
   defence of the gofpel, b. l. m g. l. Lond. by
   Grafton   ———   1547

683 Barlow's original ground of thefe Lutheran faccions, _ .2. 6 *D°*
   b. l. Lond. impr. by Cawood, 1553, Brencius's
   expoficion upon the fyxte chapter of St. John, b. l.
   Lond. by Daie   ———   1550

684 Lemnie's tovchftone of complections, b. l. Lond. imp. - 3. 6 *D°*
   by Marfhe, 1581, Faier's regiment of lyfe, b. l.
   Lond. imp. by Whytchurche   1544

685 the regiment of lyfe, with a treatife on the peftilence, - 4. _*Dr Hunter*
   b. l by Phayer   —   ib 1545

686 manipulus curatorum, m, g, l, Lond, per Wynandum _ .4. _ *D°*
   de Worde   ———   1511

687 magna carta, with divers other ftatutes, b, l, m, g, l, _ 2. 6 *Tutet*
   Lond, by Redman   1539

688 natura brevium, newly and mooft trewly corrected, - 2. _
   b, l, m, g, l, Lond, by Pynfon   1525

689 the three boukes of Tullyes offvces, both in Latyne _ .8. 6 *Nicol.*
   tonge and in Englysfhe, tranflated by Rob Whyt-
   inton, poete laureate, b, l, m, g, l, Lond, by Wynkyn de Worde   ———   1534

690 Bale's image of both churches, b, l, m, g, l, Lond, _ 3. _ *Tutet*
   imp. by Daye

691 another copy, ditto, Lond, by Eaft   _ 2. 6 *Collins*

692 Bale's actes of Englifh votaries, b, l, m, g, l, Lond, _ .4. _
   by Tifdale

693 another copy, ditto   ———   1550 _.3. 0

694 Bale's apology againft a ranke papift, b, l, m, g, l, _ 3. 6
   Lond. by Day   —   1550

695 Becon's reliques of Rome, b, l, m, g, l, with his por- _.4. 6
   trait, Lond, by Day   —   1563

696 ———s Pomaunder of prayer, b, l, m, g, l, with his _ .4. 6 *Cater*
   portrait, Lond, by Daye

E

(34)

£. s. d
17. 13. 6

713 Tyndale's parable of the wicked Mammon, b. l. 1528 —.3. _ Cater
and 2 more

714 a briefe reherfal of the doings of poyffe, in France, be- —.7.6 WH.
tween the lords fpiritual and minift·rs of the gof-
pel, Lond. imp by Harryfon, and 3 more

715 Knox's admonition to the clergy in England, b, l, m, _. 3. _D?
g, l, 1554, and 1 more

716 Turner's huntyng the Romyfhe vuolfe, b, l, m, g, l, _.4. _
and 2 more

717 a fhort defcription of antichrift to the nobility of Eng- _ .6.6 Tutet
land, b, l, m, g, l, and 2 more

718 a piftle to the chriften reader, the revelation of Anti- _ .3.6
chrift, by Brightwell, b. l. m. g. l. and one more Capt. Franklin

719 the examination of Anne Afkew, lately martyr'd in _ .8.6 Good
Smithfield by the Romifh popifh upholders, b. l. m.
g. l. with her portrait, 1546, and one more

720 puritan fermons and tracts, b. l. m. g. l. 1545, Good- - .3._ WH.
man of obedience, b. l m g. l 1558

721 Erafmus's two dialogues, called the gofpeller, &c. b. _ .3.6
l. m. g. l. and 1 more

722 Tyndale's practyfe of prelates, bl. l. and 9 other —.4._ D?
tracts

723 ftorys and prophyfis out of the holy fcriptur, with _ .4.6 D?
faire ymages, bl. l. by Coppin, 1535, Martin's
treati e of fchifme, b. l. 1578, and more

724 Gardiner's detection of the devil's fophiftrie, bl. l. _ 3._
1546, and 1 more

725 Knox's letter to the Ladie Marie regent of Scotland, _ .5._ Nicol.
m. g. l. and 1 more

726 Gardiner's de vera obedientia, b. l. m. g. l. 1553, an -.3._
anfwer to the drvilifh detection of Stephane Gardiner, b. l. m. g. . 1547

727 the hatchet of herecies, by Hofius, b. l. 1565, and _ .2.6 WH.
1 more

728 Udall's key of the holy tongue, neat, Leyd. 1593 _.2._

729 Joye's expoficion of Daniel, b l. m. g. l. Emp. at _.2.6 Tutet
Geneve, 1545

730 the nunting and finding out the Romifhe fox, b. l. m. _ 5._ WH.
g. l Bafyl, 1543

731 Hooper's declaration of the ten holy commandments, _.3.6 Dr. Hunter.
b. l. m. g. l. 1548

732 Bale's myftery of inyquete, within the hereticall ge- _.8. _ D?
nealogye of Ponce Pantolabus, b. l. m. g. l. emp.
a Geneva, by Woode, 1545

£.s.d
21.9.6

(36)

-. 4.6 733 Gualters homilies, b. l. m. g l. impr. in Sothwerke
by Trutheall, 1556

D:Hunter -. 7.6 734 Sir Thomas More's dialogue of cumfort againſt tri-
bulation, b. l. m. g. l. Antw. 1583

Brander -. 6. - 735 Pointz's teſtimonies for the ieal preſence of Chriſt's
body and blood. c. t g 1 Lóvanii ap. Foulerum,
1566, a v. ot tracts, m. g. l

D:Hunter -. 2.6 736 a godly conſultation unto the brethren and com-
panions of the chriſtian religion, by Bibliander,
b l. m. g. l. Baſil, 1542

D? -. 8.6 737 the acts ot the diſputation in the cowncell of the
empire, holden at Regenſpurg, by Coverdale. b l.
m. g. l. 1542, tracts on the ſacrament, b. l. m. g.
l. compiled by Crowley 0 548

D? -. 16. - 738 here begynr eth a lityll treatyſe ſhort and abrygyd,
ſpekynge of the art and crafte to knowe well to
dye, b l. m. g. l. no date, impr. by Pynſon Only 16 leaves.

-. 10. -739 the newe boke of juſtices of peas, b. l. impr. at Lon.
by Redman, 1538, Lumbard's duties of conſtables,
&c. b. l. m. g. l. impr Lond. by Newberie 1587

Tulet -. 4.6 740 Littleton's tenures, b. l. m. g. l. 15 6, two tracts
relating to the clergy and the laws of this realme,
b. l. m b. g. l. Lond. by Godfrey

D? -. 3.6 741 magna charta, b. l. by Geo. Feries, m. g. l. Lond.
impr. by Petyt, 1542, natura brevium, with ad-
ditions of the ſtatutes, b. l. m. g ſ. Lond. by
Petyt

WZ. -. 2.6 742 Lambard's office of the juſtices, b. l. m. g. l. Lond.
by Newberry, 1588

-. 4.6 *742 dialogus de fundamentis legum Angliæ, et de con-
ſcientia, b. l. m. g. l. 1530

Nicol -. 7. -743 the dyaloge between a docteur a d ſtudente, with newe
adycyons, b. l. m. g. l. Lond. impr. in Southwarke
by Peter Treveris, 1531

-. 3.6 744 Le Breggemen de toutez les etatez, par Owein, b. l.
m.g l. by Pynſon, 1521

Cater -. 2.6 745 Britton, cum privilego regali, b. l. m.g. l. Lond.
impr. by Redman

Dodd -. 6. - 746 magnum abbreviamentum ſtatutorum Anglie, b. l. m.
g. l. Lond impr. by Raſtell and Redman

-. 14. -747 the greate abrydgement of the ſtatutes of Englande,
Captain Franklin. untyll the 33 year of Henry the VIIIth, m g. l.
Lond. impr. by Mydylton 1542

748 Meurſii elegantiæ Latini ſermonis, & de arcana amo- — ·4· —
　　ris & veneris, *c. t. g. l.*
749 the political ſtate of Great-Britain, 57 v. bound, half *1·7·* —
　　bound, and unbound, with ſome imperfeċtions

QUARTO.

750 milk for babes, and meat for ſtrong men, a feaſt of — ·5·6 *Collins*
　　fat things, wine well refined on the lees, by James
　　Naylor, 1661, and 4 more books relating to the
　　quakers
751 Hickering Gill's miſcellaneous traċts, eſſays, ſatyrs, — ·3· — *Chapman*
　　&c. and 9 more
752 Gale's court of the gentiles, 2 v. 1672, and 4 more — ·3· — *Mann.*
753 Goodwin's pieces, 10 v. 1646, &c. — ·3· —
754 morning exerciſe againſt popery, 1675, and 9 more — ·3·6
756 Williams's concordance to the Greek Teſtament, — ·1·6 *Cater*
　　ſewed, 1767
757 Gaytons art of longevity, a poem, 1659, and 8 — ·4· — *Nicol.*
　　more
758 Eden's hiſtory of travaile in the Weſt and Eaſt In- — ·3· —*Dalby*
　　dies, *b. l.* imperfeċt, Lond. impr. by Jugge, 1577,
　　and 2 more
759 Markham's way to get wealth, 1660, Stevens's coun- — ·4· —*Nicol.*
　　try farme. by Surflet, 1606, Chambre againſt ju-
　　dicial aſtronomy, 1601
760 Luther on the Galatians, *b. l.* 1575, and 5 more — ·3· — *Chapman*
761 Martin's (Thos) unlawful marriages of prieſts, *b. l.* — ·2· — *Afflick.*
　　Lond. by Jugge, Bright's abridgement of Fox's
　　aċts and monuments, *b. l.* 1589
762 a curious Latin Bible, a MS on vellum, illuminated — ·11· —
763 the meditations of St. Bernard, *b. l.* by Wynkyn de — ·9· — *Nicol.*
　　Worde, 1496
764 the myracles of our bleſſyd lady, *b. l.* by Wynkyn — ·15·6 *Dr Hunter*
　　de Worde
765 the rule of St. Auguſtyne, *b. l.* by Wynkyn de —·11·6 *Dº.*
　　Worde, 1525
766 incipit liber qui feſtialis appellatur, *b. l.* Wynkyn — ·8· — *Nicol.*
　　de Worde, 1496
767 quatuor ſermones, *b. l.* Wynkyn de Worde, 1496 — ·11· — *Dº.*
768 Rich. Rolle Hermite of Hampull, his contemplacyons, 2· — · —
　　1506, and 5 more very curious traċts, with wood
　　cuts, *b. l.* all by Wynkyn de Worde
769 the lyfe of Jheſu Chryſte, after Bonaventure, *b. l.* — ·4·6
　　by Wynkyn de Worde, 1517

£. s. d
35. 8. 6

WH. —. 5. 6 770 Nychodemus's gofpel, *b. l.* by Wynkyn de Worde, 1532, the mofte excellent treatife of the three kynges of Coleyne, *b. l.* imperfect ditto

Gough —. 16. — 771 the martiloge in Englishe, after the ufe of the chirche of Salifbury, *b. l.* by Wynkyn de Worde, 1526

Mole —. 12. 6 772 the myrroure of golde for the fyuful foule, *b. l.* by ditto. 1526.

D° —. 9. — 773 the dyctes and the fayenges of the philofophers, *b. l. m. b. g. l.* by ditto, 1528

Thane — . 9. — 774 the courte of fapyence, *b. l. m. g. l.* by ditto, 1510

WH. —. 8. 6 775 two fermons by bifhop Fifher, called, the lamentable mornynge, *b. l. m. b g. l.* by ditto, 1509

Thane —. 5. — 776 the life of Saynte Brandon, *b. l.* and 4 more tracts by ditto

BWhite. 1. 12. — 777 Albertus Magnus de fecretis *b. l. m. g. l.* 1478, the fruyte of redemptyon, a treatife of Fyfthynge with an angle, a little treatife of the horfe, the fhepe and the g os, *b l.* by Wynkyn de Worde

Mole —. 14. — 778 fcala perfectionis, *b. l. m. g. l.* by ditto 1533

—. 7. 6 779 Fysher's feven penetencyal pfalmes of David the kinge, *b. l. m. g. l.* by ditto 1529

D° Hunt. 1. —. — 780 vita Chrifti, the life of our Lord Jefu Chryft, with wood cuts, *b. l m. g. l.* by ditto, 1529

D° 2. 2. — 781 the ordynarye of cryften men, with wood cuts, *b, l, m, g, l,* by ditto, 1506

Nicol. 2. 8. — 782 the booke intituled, the book of the ordre of chyvalry and knyghthode (one leaf wrote) *b, l, m, g, l,* by Cixton, 1485

Burnet. 3. 6. — 783 the hiftorie of Blackhardyn, fon of kinge Fryfe and princes Eglantyne, (or the proud lady of love) *b, l, m, g, l,* imperfect, by Caxton, 1485

1. 6. — 784 Milton's paradife loft and regained, 2 v. *m, b, g, l,* 1720

FOLIO.

—. 3. — 785 Heylin's cofmographv, maps, 1682, and 2 more

—. 5. — 786 Pharamond, a romance, Partnenifa, a romance

—. 4. — 787 Duff's hiftory of Scotland, Strype's annals of the reformation, 2 v.

Cater. —. 11. — 788 Holinfhed's chronicles, 2 v in 1, *b, l,* imper. 1587

—. 3. 6 789 Penn's chriftian quaker, 1664, and 2 more

—. 4. 6 790 Reynold's God's revenge againft murther, cuts, and 2 more

£. s. d
52. _ . 6

791	the works of the learned Joseph Mede,	1677	- · 4. - Cater
792	North's Plutarch's lives, Holland's Plutarch's morals		- · 11. - Cozens
793	Clarendon's history of the rebellion, v. 1ft, l, p, Oxford, 1702, Bayle's general dictionàry, v. 1ft, boards, 1734		- · 5. - Thane
794	Rushworth's historical collections, v. 1, 2, 3, l, p, 1682		- ·9. - Mann
795	Grafton's chronicle, b. l imperfect	1568	- ·4. 6 D?
796	Tindal's tranflation of the Bible, b, l, imperfect,	1549	- · 11. - Cater
797	Fairfax's Godfrey of Bulloigne, in heroic verfe,	1600	_ ·6. -
798	Sanders's phyfionomie et chiromancie, cuts (with his portrait) by Crofs, fine copy,	1653	- · 7. 6 Mann.
799	Spenfer's fairie queen, c, t, g, l, a fine copy,	1611	- ·9. 6 Cater
800	Rofs's Silius Italicus, cuts,	1661	_ ·4. - Thane
801	Ortelii theatrum orbis terrarum, cum mappis colorat, Antv.	1584	_ · 5. 6 Capt.F.Prett
802	Novum teftamentum Græcum, opera ac ftudio, J. Gregorii, Oxon.	1703	- · 4. - Chapman
803	Pope's works, 2 v. m. g. l. l. p.	1717	1. 1. -
804	——'s Homer's iliad, 6 v. in 3, m. g. l l. p. cuts,	1717	2. 11. - Cozens.
805	chronicon chronicorum, cum multis fig. b, l, Nuremberge,	1493	- · 15. - D?
806	Plutarchi vita Latine, per Nicolaum Jenfon, Venet,	1478	2. 3. -
807	M. Antonii Sabellici, in tris triginta fuos, rerum venetar, libros epitomæ, m, g, l, Venet	1487	1. 5. Hayes
808	Biblia facra, m, g, l,	1478	1. 17. -
809	fancti ambrofii epifcopi in corpus evangelii fancti luce evangelifte, m, g, l, Auguftae	1476	3. 3. Dr. Hunter
810	Laurentii Vallenfis de Linguæ Latinæ, m, g, l, Venet	1486	- · 11. - Cater
811	the Holy Bible, b, l, Lond, imp, bv Barker	1640	- · 7. 6 Morgan
812	the fhepheard's kalender, b, l, very fair, and neat, cuts	1656	- · 14. - Gough
813	the arte or crafte to lyve well and to dye well, b, l, with wood cuts, very neat, · Lond, emprent'd by Wynkyn de Worde,	1505	1. 18. - Pratt
814	Sir Thomas More's fupply cacyon of foulys, againft the fupplycacyon of beggars, b, l, m, g, l,		- · 17. Dr. Hunter
815	the cuftomes of the cyte of London, b, l, m, g, l.		3. 16. Shropshire
816	the defence of peace, tranflated out of Laten in Englyfshe with the kynges moft gracyous privilege, b, l, m, g, l, impr. by Wyer,	1535	1. 10. Mason

79. 1. –

Canter   *1. 2. –*   817 the auncient hiftorie and only trew and fyncere cronicle of the warres betwixte the Grecians and the
Troyans, b, l, m, g, l, by John Ludgate Moncke
of Burye, Lond, imp, by Marfhe   1555

Nicol.   *2. 14. –*   818 a dyalogve of dives and pauper that is to faye the ryche
and the Poore, with wood cuts, b, l, m, g, l, emp,
by Wynkyn de Worde   1496

D°   *1. 17. –*   819 Bochas's fall of princes and dyvers other nobles, with
wood cuts, b, l, m, g. l, imp, by Tottell,   1554

Shropfhire   *4. 1. –*   820 the noble and joyous booke, entyteled a treatife of
the byrthe, lyfe and actes of Kynge Arthur and his
noble knyghtes of the round table, b, l, with wood
cuts, m, g, l, Lond imp, by Copland

D°.   *3. 6. –* 821 the hiftory of the moofte noble and valyaunt knyght
Arthur of Lytell Brytayne, b, l, m, g, l, by Cop-
lande

B. White.   *4. 10. –* 822 the right pleafaunt and goodly hiftorie of the foure
fonnes of Aymon, with wood cuts, b, l, m, g, l,
by Copland,   1532

£ 96. 11 –

End of the Fifth Day's Sale.

Sixth Day's Sale,

TUESDAY, APRIL 2, 1776.

OCTAVO and DUODECIMO.

£. s. d

824 LETTRES perfannes, and 15 more — 2.6
825 Hickefii Ling. Vett. Septenttionalium Thefauri, —10.6
1708, and 9 more
826 Ockam tractatus, de Sacramento Altaris, bl. let. ap. —9.6
Petit, 1513, and 7 more
827 Suetonii opera, apud. Gryphium, 1551, and 5 more —1.6
828 Biblia facra cum Concordatitys veteris, cum fig. 1519, —2. 6
and 5 more
829 Lee's effay on annuities and chances, 1738, and 3 — 2._
more
830 Whifton's theory of the earth. Woodward's natural —4._
hiftory of the earth, 1695
831 Barclay's apology for the Quakers, l. p. King's mif- _ 2._
cellanies, l. p.
832 Ridley's review of Phillips's life of Cardinal Pole, _ .2..
1766, and 2 more
833 A relation of the earthquake at Lima, in 1746. and —.3._
1 more
834 The mafque, a collection of Englifh, Scotch, and — .1.6 Chapman
Irifh fongs, and 2 more
835 Crofby's hiftory of the Englifh baptifts, 4 vols. 1738 —.2._
836 Wit's commonwealth, m b 1598. Wit's theatre of —.3._ Nicol.
the little world, m b. 1599
837 Luther's articles of the Chriften Faythe, bl. m. b —.2.6 WH.
1548. Bradforde's godlye treatife of prayer, b
l. m. b. impor. by J. Wight, and 2 more
838 Ponet's notable fermon, b. l. m. b. 1550 St. Chry- —1.6 D.°
foftom's fermon, b. l. m. b. impr. by Berthelet,
1542, and 2 more
839 The fupplication of the poore Commons; t which — 4._ D.° Wright.
is added, The fupplication of beggars, b. l m, g. l.
1524. and 2 more
840 The boke of Wifdome, called the flower of vertue, —.3._ Reed.
by Larke, b. l. m. b. 1565, and 1 more
F

£. s. d
2. 17. –

Recd   – *2. 6* 841 Erafmus's epiftle fente unto Conradus Pelicanus, concerning the facrament, b. l. 1554. Bellum Eraf-
mi, tranflated into Englyfhe, b. l. m. g. l. by Berthelet,   1534

Gayfly   – 2. – 842 The ordenarye for all faythfull Chryftians to leade a
godly lyfe, with wood cuts, b. l. m. g. l. Lond.
impr. by Scoloker. The parable of the wicked
Mammon, b l. m. g l.   1536

Wt   –. *3. 6* 843 The fermons of Barnadine Ochyne, b. l. Lond. impr.
by John Day. Prayers or medytacions, collected
out f holy woorkes, b. l. m. b by Waylande, 1545

D°   –. *3.* – 844 Here begynnethe the lanterne of lyght, b. l. m. g. l.
Lond impr. by Redman De contemptu mundi,
tranflated into Englyfhe, b. l. m. g. l. by Berthelet,   1533

  – *3.* – 845 The fhelde of falvacion, bl. l. m. g. l. impr. by Robert Wyer. A frutefull treatyfe, teachynge the
waye of dyenge well, bl. l. m. g. l. by Lupfete,
impr. by Berthelet,   1541

D°   –. *2.* – 846 Tyndall and Lambert on the facraments, b. l. m. g. l.
Lond. 1538. The examplayre upon the paynes of
Hell, b. l. m. g. l. impr. by Wyer

Cozens   –. *1. 6* 847 An introduction to wifdome, by Vives, tranflated
into Englyfhe by Moryfine, bl. l. m. g. l. by Ber-
thelet, 1544, and 1 more

D.ʳ Wright . *3.* – 848 The troubled man's medicine, by Hughe, b. l. m. g. l.
impr. by Rogers. A fpirituall perie, teaching all
men to love and embrace the Croffe, b. l. m. g. l.
impr. by Elde, and 1 more

  – *4. 6* 849 Hooper on the ten holy commaundementes, b. l. m. g. l.
1550. Leaver's fruitfull fermon, in Poule's churche,
bl. l. m. g. l.   1550

D°   –. *4.* – 850 De Neutralibus & Medicis. grofly Inglyfhed, jacke
of both fides, b. l. m. g. l. imperf. impr. by Har-
rifon, 1562. Tracts concerning purgatorye and
the facraments, by Frith, Raftell, and More, b. l.
m. g. l. impr. in the Yare   1548

Cozens   –. *3.* – 851 The feven penytencyall pfalmes of Davyd the Kynge,
b. l. m. g. l. impr. by Marfhe, 1550 how fupe-
riour powers ought to be obey'd of their fubjects,
by Goodman, m. g. l.   1558

Gough   –. *8.* – 852 The Salifbury Prymer, b. l. m. g. l. with cuts, impr.
at Roven,   1537

Wt.   –. *6.* – 853 King Edward the 6th's Common Prayer, bl. l. Thr.
New Teftament, bl. l, with Tindall's notes

  –. *6. 6* 854 The imitation, or following of Chrift, by Thomas
Kempife, a Dutchman, bl. l. m. g. l. impr. by
Denham, 1567, the following of Chrift, with the

£. s. d
5 . 9 . 6

golden epiftle of St. Barnarde, b. l. m. g. l. by
Cawoxd, 1556

855 The pandeftes of the evangelical lawe, by Paynell, — . *1. 6 Gayfly*
bl. l. 1553. The workes of Thomas Lupfet, bl. l.
Lond. 1546

856 The Cmmon Prayer Book, bl. l m. g. l. by Seres. — *3. 6 Hayes*
1565. The obedyence of a Criften man, bl l.
m. g. l. Lond. impr. by Coplande,   1561

857 A playne and godly expofition of the comune, crede, — . *3.*
by Erafmus, bl. l. m, g. l. impr. by Redman.
Taverneı s common places of fcripture, bl. l. m. b.
1553

858 An abridgmente of the Olde Teftament, in verfe, — . *7. 6*
by Samuel, b. l. c. t. g. l.   by Seres, 1569

859 The Newe Teftament, by Tyndall, imperf. bl. l. — . *4. 6 WH.*
m. g. l.

860 The Prymer of Salifbury, with cuts, b l. m. g. l. — . *6. — Gough*
printed by Johan Gowghe

861 A dialogue of Dives and Pauper, that is to fay, the — . *6. 6 Hayes*
ryche and the poore, b. l. m. g. l. impr. by Ber-
thelet,   1536

862 The apologye of Sir Thomas More, Knyght, b. l. — . *6. 6*
m. g. l. printed by Raftell,   1533

863 A treatife of fchemes and tropes, for the better un- — . *3. 6 Edward*
derftanding of good authors, by Erafuus, b. l.
m g. l. by Day, 1550   Traheron's expofition of
St. John's gofpel, m b.   1605

864 The Newe Teftament, bl l. m. g. l. by Berthelet — . *8. 6 F*

865 Becon's reliques of Rome, with his portrait, b. l. — . *5. — Hayes*
m. g l. by Day,   1563

866 The Newe Teftament, with the portrait of Edward — . *11. —*
the 6th, bl. l. m. g. l impr. by Jugge,   1562

867 Joye's expofycion of Daniel, bl. l. m. g. l. impr. by — . *3. — D°*
Raynalde,   1550

868 Hoper's feven fermons,, b. l. m. g. l. Lond. impr. — . *4. —*
by Tifdale, *with his Confifsion of Faith* .   1559

869 Archtifhop Cranmer's catechifms, cuts, b. l. m. g. l. — . *13. — F*
by Lynne,   1548

870 The hunting of purgatorye to death, by Veron, bl. l. — . *5. — Edwards*
m. g. l. by Tyfdale,   1561

871 The enfamples of vertue and vice, Englifhed by — . *7. — Nicol*
Paynell, b. l. m. g. l. impr. by Tifdale,   1561

872 Mayfter Hugh Latimer's fermons, bl. l. m. g. l. — . *7. 6 Hayes*
impr. by John Day

873 Udall's apothegmes, that is to faie, quicke, wittie — . *11. Nicol*.
fayinges, of emperours, kings, philofophiers, &c,
b. l m , g. l. Typis Ricardi Grafton,   1542

l.s d

11.12.—

Edwards —. 4.6 874 The pithy and moſt notable ſayinges cf al ſcripture
by Paynell, b 1. m. g. l.   1550

Collins —. 3.6 875* The New Teſtament in Engliſhe, wyth the tranſla-
tion of Eraſmus. in Latin, bl. 1.   1550

—. 6. — 875 the Turkyſhe chronicles, by Aſhton, b. 1. m. g. 1.
impr. by Whitchurch   1516

876 the eight bookes of Xenophon, tranſlated by Bercker,
b. 1. m. g. 1.   1567

Reed. —. 4.6 877 the golden boke of Marcus Aurelius the Empereur,
b, 1, m, g, 1,   1559

B.White. —. 15.6 878 ſonges and ſonnetes, by the Earl of Surrey, b, 1, m,
g, 1, Lond. imp. by John Windet   1585

Nicol. —. 5.6 879 the ſentences of Terence, Lat. and Eng. b, 1, m, g, 1,
by Berthelet, 1560, Langley's abridgement of the
notable worke of Polidore Vergile, b, 1, m, b, 1551

W.White. —. 3. —880 the circes of John Baptiſta Gello, tranſlated by Iden,
b, 1, m, g, 1, impr. by Cawoode   1557

Cater —. 6. — 881 the boke named the governour, by Sir Thomas Elyet,
Knt. b, 1, m, g, 1, impr. by Berthelet   1546

WH. —. 5.6 882 a booke called in Latyn enchiridion militis chriſtiani,
and in Engliſh, the manuel of the cnriſten knyght,
by Eraſmus, b, 1, m, g, 1, by Wynkyn de Worde,
1533

Hayes — 4.6 882 the image of God, in which the right knowledge of
God is diſcloſed, by Hutchinſon, b, 1, m, b, impr.
by Day, 1560, the ymage of both paſtoures, made
Englyiſhe by John Veron, b, 1, m, g, 1,   1550

D' —. 3.6 883 the ſhippe of aſſured ſafetie, by Cradocke, b, 1, neat,
1 ond impr. by Bynneman, 1572, Watſon's two no-
table ſermons. b, 1, imperſect, neat, imp. by Cawood,
1554

WH. —. 9. — 884 Peryn's ſpirituall exercyſes and gooſtly meditations,
b, 1, impr. by Waley, 1557, ancient tracts, humble
petition of the commons to Queen Elizabeth, &c.
Cranmer's confutation of unwritten verityes, Bate-
man's diſplaying the familie love of lyfe of Arch.
Parker, b, 1,   1574

Hayes —. 6. — 885 a ſpyrytuall and mooſt precyouſe pearle, teachyng all
men to love and imbrace the croſſe, b, 1, m, g, r,
impr. by Lynne, 1550, a battell between vertues
and vices, englyiſh'd by Fleming, impr. by Denham

Nicol. —. 10.6 886 expoſitions upon the prophetes Aggeus and Abdyas,
b, 1, m, g. 1, 1562, the true copye of a prolog,
wrytten about 200 yeres paſte, by John Wycklife,

£. s d
16. 9. 6

called the pathwaye to perfect knowlege, b, l, m,
g, l, with his portrait, Lond. impr. by Crowley,
                                                    1550
887 a neceſſary doctrine and erudition for any chryſten   4. -
    man, b, l, m, g, l,   1534
888 here beginneth the booke of Reynarde the foxe, con- - 12. _D.ͬ Chauna
    taining divers goodly hiſtoryes, b, l, m, g, l, Lond.
    impr. by Gaultier   1550
889 pithy pleaſaunt and profitable workes of Maiſter Skel- 1 3 _Nicol
    ton, b, l, m, g, l, Lond impr. by Marſhe   1562
890 epitaphes, epigrams, ſonges and ſonets, by Turber- - 9 _
    ille, b, l, m, b, by Denham   1570
891 the profitable arte of gardening, by Hill, b, l, m, g, l, - 7. 6 Barclet
    by Marſhe   1568
892 the fardle of factions, by Watreman, b, l, m, g, by - 17. _ Nicol
    Kingſtone   1555
893 the conqueſts of Tamburlaine, the Scythian ſhepheard, 1 4 _Maſon
    b, l, m, g, l, printed by Inones   1590
894 the hiſtorye of Quintus Curtius, by Brende, b. l. neat, _. 4. _Gayſloy
                                           Lond. 1592
895 a compendious and moſt marveylous hiſtory of the - 5. 6 Tulet
    Jewes, by Ben Gorion, b, l, m, g, l,   1561
896 another copy, b, l, m, g, l,   1575 - 5. -
897 the bokes of Salomon, b, l, m, g, l, Lond. impr. by _ 5. 6 Cater
    Copland   1551
898 the zodiacke of life, by Barnabe Googe, b, l, m. g, l, - 7. _ WH
    by Denham   1572
899 a pleaſant diſcourſe of the whole arte of phiſiognomie, _ 7. _Tutet
    with wood cuts, b, l, m, b,
900 the political ſtate of Great Britain, 20 odd v. bound - 9 _ WH.
                        QUARTO.
901 Middleton's miſcellaneous tracts, ſew'd, 1752, and - 2. 6 D.ͦ
    two more
902 Hughes's abridgment of acts and ordinances, 1657, — 1. 6
    and 4 more
903 Cooper s cnronicle, b. l. 1565, and 1 more   — 4. 6
904 Sigiberti chronicon, 1513, and 3 more   — 4. 6
905 Calvin on the three evangeliſts, 1584, Wicklifee on _ 3. 6
    the ſacrament, 1612, and 2 more
906 Hill s thoughts on God and nature, in anſwer to Lord — 4. -
    Bolingbroke   1755
907 the letters of Cranmer, Hooper, Ridley, &c. b. l. _ 5. 6 Good.
    1564, newe teſtament, b. l. 1612, and 1 more
908 Guevaia's golden epiſtles, b. l. printed by Newberie, — 3. 6
    1534, Agrippa's vanitie of artes and ſciences, b. l.

£ s. d
24.18.6

1575, hiftory of Palmerin D'Oliva, Emper. of Conftantinople, b. l. imperfect

—. *1. 6* 909 Lipfius de Machinis, cum figuris, Antv. 1596, Whitney's emblemes, imperfect

—. *3. 6* 910 opufculum plane divinum de Mortuarum refurrectione, in quatuor linguis, a Clerco, Lond. by Herforde, 1545, and 3 more

—.*5.*— 911 Batman's doome warning to the judgement, b. l. imperfect, moral philofophie of the ancient fages, b. l. imperfect, a d 6 more

—. *2. 6* 912 cours de philofophie, par Regis, 3 vols. Amft. 1691, and 1 more

B.White —. *4.* — 913 Merline's life and ftrange prophecies, by Heywood, 1641

—. *5. 6* 914 la henriade de Mr. Voltaire, avec fig. g. l. Lond. 1728

—. *2.* — 915 Glover's Leonidas, a poem, boards 1737

Gayfly —. *7. 6* 916 Milton's paradife regain'd, fine y bound 1720

B White —. *7. 6* 917 Barckley's felicitie of man, a fine copy, c. t. g. l. 1598

—. *6.* — 918 life of Sir Thomas More, m. g. l

Connaught . *7.* — 919 Lambarde's perambulation of Kent, a fair copy 1596

—. *3.* — 920 puritan tracts, by Powell and others, m. g. l. 1605

WWhite —. *2. 6* 921 ditto, by various authors, m g. l. 1607

—. *1.* — 922 —— canne neceffitie of feparation, m. g. l. 1634

Gayly —. *2.* — 923 ditto, Huntley of prelate tyranny, m. g. l. 1637

Cater —. *4.* — 924 ditto, Sion's plea againft the prelacy, cuts, m. g. L. 1628

—. *3. 6* 925 —— admonition to the parliament, anno 1570 to 71, m. g. l. 1617

D? —. *3.* — 926 —— Baftwick's litany with the anfwers, m. g. l. 1637

Mechb.m —. *2.* — 927 —— Whetenhall's difcourfe of the abufes in churches, m. g. l. 1606

—. *1. 6* 928 —— Johnfon againft Jacob's defence, b. l. m. g. l. 1600

Edwards . *1. 6* { 929 —— the Brownift defence, and other tracts 1604
—— Englifh popifh ceremonies difputed 1637

—. *1. 6* 930 —— fome againft Penry, 1588, the courfe of conformitie 1622

WWhite —. *2. 6* 931 —— four by Cartwright and others, m. g. l. 1599

Bartlet —. *16.* — 932 Martin Mar prelate, oh read over John Bridges for its worthy worke, hay any worke for ccoper, printed in Europe, not far from fome of the bouncing prieftes, b. l. very fcarce, m. g. l.

—. *2.* — 933 Goodwin's tracts, right and might well met, &c. &c. m. b. 1648

£. s. d.
29. 9. 6

934 Prynne's new difcovery of the prelates tyranny, with — 5. D.Chauncy
four portraits, m g, l. 1641
935 —— antipathie of the Englifh lordly prelacie, m. — 2. — D.°
g. l. 1641
936 Latymer's frutefull fermons, b. l. m. g. l. Lond. by — 10. 6 Gray
Daye 1578
937 Bullinger's 100 fermons upon the apocalips of Jefu — 5. — Cater
Chrift, b. l. m. g. l., by Daye 1561
938 Bp Bonner's homilies, b. l. m. g. l. printed by Ca- — 6. 6 Hayes
wood
939 St. Chrifoftome upon the epiftle of St. Paul, b. l. m. — 4. —
g. l. by Bynneman 1581
940 the pathway to the pulpit, or the practife of preaching — 5. 6
englifhed. by Ludham, b. l. m. g. l. by Eaft 1577
941 a poftill of certaine epiftles, by Golding, b l. m. g. l. — 4. 6
impr. by Bynneman 1570
942 book of homilies, b. l. very neat, g. l, Lond. impr. by — 8. 6 F.
Jugge 1572
943 Martin of prieftes unlawfull mariages, b. l. m. g. l. by — 6. — Edward,
Caly, 1554, a defence of prieftes mariages againft
Martin, b. l. m. g. l. by Jugge
944 Luther's fermons, b, l, m, g, l, Lond. impr. by Vou- — 10. — Nicol
troullier, 1581, Luther's expofition upon Peter and
Jude, b, l, m, g, l, impr. by Veale 1581
945 Calvine's 13 fermons, neat, 1579, the finner's guide, — 4. — Hayes
tranflated by Meres, m, g, l, 1598
946 the fermon which chrift made going to Emaus, b, l, — 4. 6 Mich.m
m, g, l, Lond, imp. by Daye 1578
947 the epiftles and gofpels, by Taverner, b. l. m. g. l. — 7. 6 Nicol.
Lond. imp. by Banks
948 Crowley's fubtile fophriftrie of Dr. Watfon which he — 3. 6 Cater
ufed in his 2 fermons, preached before Queen Mary,
b. l. c. t. g. l. by Denham, 1569
949 Crowley's defen e of thofe Englifhe writers and — 3. 6 WH.
preachers which Cerbarus the three headed dog of
hell chargeth with falfe doctrine &c. b. l. m. b.
Lond imp. by Binneman 1556
950 Bp. Hooper's expofitions upon the Pfalms, b. l. neat — 1. 6 White.
1580, Knewftub's lectures upon Genefis, b. l. m. b.
1578
951 Marbeck's booke of notes and common places, b. l. — 2. 6 Cater
m. b. by Eaft, 1581
952 the pfalter and collects, b. l. m. b. printed, by Seres, — 5. — D.°
pfalmorum omnium, b. l. m. g. l. imp. by Berthe-
let 1534
953 Keltridge's expofition upon Luke M. B, 1578 and 3 — 8 6 WH.
more

£. s. d
34. 17. 6　　　　　(48)

Thane — 7. 6 954 ftultifera navis, cum fig. imperfect

D.ʳHunter — 2. 6 955 practica in arte chirurgica copiofa, per Vigo, b. l. m.
　　　　　　　　　g. l. Lugd, 1512

Hayes — 2. 6 956 Bertruccii opera medica, b, l, m, g, l. Lugd　1509

— 3. 6 957 a devout treatyfe called the tree and 12 frutes of the
　　　　　　Holy Goofte, imp. by Coplande,　　　　　1539

Thane — 4. _ 958 de contemptu mundi, by Thomas Paynall, imp by
　　　　　　Berthelet, injunccions given by Edward the Vith,
　　　　　　to the clergie and laietie, b, l, m, b, Lond, imp,
　　　　　　by Grafton　　　　　　　　　　　　　　1547

D.ʳHunter — 17. — 959 Whitintoni, grammatices de nominum generibus, b,
　　　　　　l, m, b, Wynkyn de Worde

Dᵒ — 6. 6 960 quinta recognitio at 9 additio ad gramaticen fulpici-
　　　　　　anam b, l, m, b, ap, Wynkyn de Worde

Dᵒ — 13. 6 961 Roberti Wakefeldi oratio de laudibus utilitate,
　　　　　　Ling. Arab. Chald Hebraice, m, b, Lond. ap.
　　　　　　Winandum de worde,　　　　　　　　　1523

— 1. — 9⁶ 2 Joannis Defpauterii ninivite fyntaxes, m, b, Argent
　　　　　　Schurerii　　　　　　　　　　　　　　1515

Thane — 15. — 963 fynonimi magiftri Johannis de Garlandia, cum expo-
　　　　　　fitione magiftra galfride anglici, nuperimo correcti,
　　　　　　& londinenfis impreffa, per Winandum de Worde
　　　　　　　　　　　　　　　　　　　　　　　　1505

Dᵒ — 2. _ 964 Jo, fulpitii Verulani de Octo Partibus orationis libellus
　　　　　　utiliffemus, b, l, m. b.　　　　　　　　1514

Dampier — 1. 6 965 Joː Difpauterii ninivite rudimenta grammatices, m, b,
　　　　　　　　　　　　　　　　　　　　　　　　1512

F. 1. 2. — 966 vulgaria, guil, Hormanni cæfarifburgenfis, apud inclv-
　　　　　　tam Londini urbem, m, b, per Winai dum de Worde
　　　　　　　　　　　　　　　　　　　　　　　　1530

— 2. 6 967 Ciceronis Rhetoricum, m, b. excubat hero Alopectus
　　　　　　1522, Tufculanæ quaftiones, m, b, Bafil ap, Fro-
　　　　　　benium,　　　　　　　　　　　　　　　1523

— 2. 6 958 Epiftolæ erafmi ad Eriditos & Horum ad illum, m,
　　　　　　g, l, 1518, Erafmus de Octo Partium orationes, m,
　　　　　　b.　　　　　　　　　　　　　　　　　1517

Edwards. — 5. — 969 elucidarius carminum & hiftoriarum, feu vocab poet,
　　　　　　Fabulas, m, g, l　　　　　　　　　Paris 1507

— 5. — 970 expofitio beati Gregorii Pape fuper cantica canti orum
　　　　　　m, g, l,　　　　　　　　　　　　　　1498

— 6. — 971 Gregorii Pape, in fceptem pfalmus peneten iales, b.
　　　　　　l m, g, l, 1508. de vita miraculis Patrum itali-
　　　　　　curum & de eternitate animarum, b, l, m g, l,
　　　　　　　　　　　　　　　　　　　　　　　　1506

£. s. d

41.7. -

972 The Forme and maner of makyng and confecratyng, _. 4.6
Arch Bifhops, Bifhops, Prieftes and Deacons, bl. l.
neat, very fcarce, impr. by Grafton   1549

973 The Boke of Comfort, called in Laten Boetius _.2.6
de Confolatione, Philofophie, by me D. Thos.
Richard Monke of Taveftok, b. l. m. g. l.   1525

974 The 15 Bookes of Ovid Metamorphofis, by Ar. Goid- -.12. 6
ing, bl. l. m. g. l. impr. by Seres   1567

975 The 13 Bukes of Eneados of Virgil, by Gawin Doug- 1.11.6
las, bl. l. m. g. l.   Lond. 1553

976 The Poefies of Geo. Gafcoigne, Efq. b. l. m. g. l. .1. 13. _
impr. by Bynneman   1575

977 The Hyftory and Queftions of Kynge Boccus and S;-_. 18. _
drake, b. l. m. g. l. (9 pages wrote) printed by
Godfrey   1510

978 Heywood's Parable of the Spider and Flie, with wood 1. 14. _
cuts, with his Portrait, bl. l. m. g. l. impr. by
Powell   1556

979 The Decades of the newe World, or Weft India, by- 73 _
Eden, b. l. m. g. l.   Lond. impr. by Jugge 1555

980 Hardyng's Chronicle of England, in Profe and Verte, -.10.6
b. l. imperfect, printed by Grafton

981 Incipit Liber qui Feftivalis appellantur, b. l. 2 pages -.9. _
wro e, printed by Caxton   1496

982 Hore beatiffime Virginis Marie ad Legit. Sarifburi- -.9. _
enfis, Ecclef. ritum cum figuris, g. l. Paris per
Regnault   1536

983 Tenores novelli Littleton, b. l. m. b. Lond. per lo. 2. 15. _
Lettou & de Machlinia

984 Sixty-four Portraits of the King of France, from Pha- - 16. _
ramond to Lewis XIV. de l'Armeffin fculp. 1714,
m. g. l.

F O L I O.

985 St. Ambrofii opera tom. 1ft and 3d, and two more —. 8.6
986 Milton's Political Works, Vol. I. Strype's Annals, -.9. 6
Vol. I. and II.

987 Calvin's Sermons, 1574. Stebbing's Polemical Tracts — 2. 6

1727

988 Froiffart' Chronicles of England, France, &c. Vol. 1ft. -.12.6
one leaf wanting

989 Ciceronis Epiftolæ Affentio, 1505. Valerius Maxi- -. 3. _
mus ab. Affentio, 1510. Fabii Quintiliani orat.
Inftitut. ab. Affenfio   1516

2. 6. –   990 Rapin's Hiſtory of England, 3 vol. by Tindal, with
               Heads and Monuments, – by Vertue, &c. 1732.
               N. B. The Heads bound ſeparate

1. 12. – 991 The Myrrour: and Dyſcrypcyon of the Worlde with
               many Mervaylies, bl. l. with many wood cuts,
               m. g. l. by Andrewe

–. 12. – 992 The Vertuoſe Boke of Diſtylacyon, bl. l. m. g. l. by
               Andrewe   1527

–. 10. – 993 The Brytiſh Mouarchie, pertaining to the Art of Na-
               vigation, m. g. l. printed by Daye   1577

2. –. –   994 the hyſtory ſege and deſtruccyon of Troye, with wood
               cuts, by John Lydgate Moncke of Bury, b. l. m.
               g l. (two leaves wrote) impr. by Pynſon   1513

–. 6. – 995 the yere bookes for 1534, 5, 6 and 7, bl. l. m. b. per
               Pynſon

2. 4. – 996 Chaucer's Canterburie Tales, b. l. m. g. l. with wood
               cuts, printed by Pyuſon

–. 4. – 997 a treatyſe f the donation or gyfte and endowment of
               poſſeſſyons gyven and graunted unto Sylveſter, pope
               of Rhome, bl. l. impr. by Thos. Godfray

–. 15. – 998 Jherome's roble experyence of the virtuous handy
               worke of ſurgeri, with wood cuts, bl. l. m. g. l.
               impr. by Treveris   1525

1. 15. – 999 the booke of the cuſtomes of the cite of London,
               bl. l. m. g. l. ſuppoſed to be printed before Mid-
               ſummer, 1503

1. 11. 6 1000 the right pleſaunt and goodly hiſtorie of the foure
               ſonnes of Aimon, verie pleaſaunt to rede, with
               wood cuts, 1 leaf wrote, bl. l. m. g. l. impr. by
               Copland   1554

2. 15. – 1001 the grete herball, bl. l. with wood cuts, m. g. l. im-
               printed in Southwarke by P. Treveris   1529

2. 2. – 1002 the lyfe of Seynt Katheryne of Sene, a fine copy,
               bl. l. m. b. printed by Wynkyn de Worde   1519

2. 3. – 1003 the pilgrymage of Perfeccyon, a fine copy, with
               wood cuts, b. l. m. g. l. by Wynkyn de Worde
                                                            1531

1. 5 1004 the floure of the commandementes of God, bl. l.
               with wood cuts, m. g. l. Wynkyn de Worde 1521

3. –. – 1005 fructus temporum; the ceſcrypcyon of Englonde,
               Wailes, Scolonde and Irlonde, bl. l. neat, impr.
               by Wynkyn de Worde   1498

2. 17. – 1006 Grafton's Chronicle of England, 2 vol. b. l. a fine
               copy, m. g. l.   1569

1007 Linſchoten's

£. s. d
83. 5. 6

1007 Linfchoten's voyages into the Eafte and Weft Indies, bl. l. with fine maps and cuts, a fine copy, m. g. l. Lond. printed by Wolfe 1598- *1. 10. —*

1008 a new comedye in Englyfhe in maner of an enterlude, ryght elegant and full of craft of rethoryk, &c. b. l._ *1. 10. —* printed by Raftell

1009 three dyalogues, viz. of the mervelous exiftens of God, of the immortalyte of manny's foule, and of purgatory, bl. l. by Raftell 1530 — — *. 5. —*

1010 the boke of the lyeng wydow Edyth, bl. l. m. b. by Raftell 1525- *3. 16. —*

1011 the confutacyon of Tyndales anfwere, by Syr Thos. More, 2 vol. bl. l. a fine copy, m. g. l. prented by Raftell 1532- — *12. 6*

1012 a dyaloge of Syr Thos. More, touching the peftylent fecte of Luther and Tyndale, b. l. m. g. l. by John Raftell 1530- *1. — . —*

1013 the paftyme of people; the cronyc'es of dyvers realmys, with heads to Richard III. b. l. m. g. l. _ *8. 15. —* by John Raftell

1014 the boke of fame made by Gefferey Chaucer, b. l.. *2. 15. —* emprynted by Caxton, no date

1015 The boke of Eneydos compyled by Vyrgyle, b. l, m. b. printed by Caxton 1490- *. 5. 12. 6*

1016 the boke called Caton, tranflated into Englyfshe, bv Mayfter Banet Burgh late archdcken of Colcheftre, b. l. m. g. l. by Caxton 1483- *3. 13. 6*

1017 Here begynneth the myrrour of the world or thymage of the fame, with wood cuts, b. l. m. g. l. printed by Caxton 1480- *4. 17. —*

1018 the boke entytiled Tullie of olde age and frendfhyp, b. l. m. g. l. feven leaves wrote, printed by Caxton 1481 - *1. 14. —*

1019 fpeculum vitæ Crifti; or the myrroure cf the bleffed lyf of Jhefu Chryfte, b. l. m. g. l. with wood cuts,- *3. 3. —* by Caxton

1020 liber feft valis, b. l. m. g. l. printed by Caxton 1483 *3. — . —*

1021 the canterburie tales, made by Maiftre Chaucer, witn wood cuts, firft edit. bl. l. m. g. l. made perfect *4. — . —* by MSS, printed by Caxton

1022 the cronicles of Englonde, b. l. m. g. l. made perfact by MSS, printed by Caxton 1480- *4. 5. —*

1023 the Polycronicon, bl. l. m. g. l. made perfect by MSS, printed by Caxton 1482- *3. 3. —*

1024 the

£. s. ?
5. 15. 6.   1024 the legende, named in Latyn, legeuda aurea, that is
to saye in Englyfshe the golden legende, bl. l. m.
g. l. with wood cuts, by Caxton   1483

End of the Sixth Day's Sale.

SEVENTH DAY'S SALE,

WEDNESDAY, APRIL 3.

Octavo and Duodecimo.

£. s. d.   LOT.

—. 5. 6 1025 La vie & les actions de Adm¹ al de Ruyter, and 22
more

—. 3. 6 1026 Monumenta vetustatis Kempiana, and 10 wore

—. 1. — 1027 Magua charta, cum statutis antiqua, typis ap. Tote-
lum, 1556, and 5 more

—. 3. — 1028 Brevis Inftitut. ad Chrift. pietatem, a Sebaftiano, cum
fig. 1550, and 9 more

—. 5. — 1029 Wotton's lives, letters, poems, &c. 1672, and 9 more

—. 1. 6 1030 Vicars's Virgil, 1632, and 10 more

—. 4. — 1031 Whichcote's fermons, vol. 1ft and 2d, 12mo, and
15 more

—. 1. 6 1032 Dodwell on the foul, and 18 more on ditto

—. 4. 6 1033 The Englifh martyrologe, lives of faintes, 1608, and
24 more

—. 6. 6 1034 Twenty-two black letter books, imperfect, fome fcarce

—. 1. 6 1035 Thirteen books and pamphlets relating to the
puritans

—. 4. — 1036 The political ftate of Great Britain, 20 odd volumes
half bound

—. 2. — 1037 Dering's fermons, &c. and 5 more

—. 5. — 1038 A commentarie upon the booke of Proverbes, M.G.L.
printed by Field, 1592 and 7 more

—. 1. 6 1039 Evans's admonitions to the minifters of Englande,
1565, and 4 more

—. 7. — 1040 Puritan's fermons and tracts, m. g. l. 1585, and
4 more

1041 Penri's

£. s. d
8. 10. 6

1041 Penri's application to the high court of parliament) _ . 5. _ *Tutet*
m. g. l. 1589, and 4 more

1042 Camdeni Britannia, (with his portrait by Marſhall, - . 2. _ *Fox.*
Londini, per Newbery 1589, and 4 more

1043 Plinii hiſtoria naturalis, ludg. ap. juntas 1561, and - . 2. _
4 more

1044 Magna Charta cum ſtat. antiq. ap. tottellum 1556,- . 1. 6 *B.White*
and 2 more

1045 a dialogue between a docteur and ſtudent, b. l. m. _ . 4. 6 *Tutet*
g. l. impr. by Redman 1531, and 2 more

1046 Littleton's expoſicions of the terms of the laws of - . 7. _ *Bartlett*
England. c. t. g. l. per Rich. Totell 1567, and
3 more

1047 Aſkham's lytel herbal of the properties of herbes, &c. - . 9. _ *Tutet*
b. l. m. b. impr. by Wm. Powell 1550, and
4 more

1048 Hutten's treatyſe of the wood guaiacum, that healeth - . 4. 6
the Frenche pockes, bl. l. m. b. Lond. by Berthe-
let 1536, and 3 more

1049 Bullein's government of health, bl. l. impr. by - 5. 6 *Miles*
J. Daye 1559, and 3 more

1050 Regimen ſanitanis ſalerni, by Paynell, b. l. impr. _ 4. _ *Bartlett*
by Wele. 1557. Baneſter's choice of medicines,
bl. l. impr. by Orwin, 1589

1051 Phaire's regiment of life, bl. l. m. g. l. impr. by - . 9. _ *B White*
whitchurch, 1551 and 3 more

1052 Foxe's ſermons at Paules Croſſe, bl. l. impr. by - . 3. 6 *Tutet*
Daye, 1575, and 5 more

1053 Two curious tracts of Martin Marplelate, very ſcarce - . 10. _

1054 Chriſtopherſon's exhortation to all men to take hede - . 5. _ *W.*
and beware of rebellion, b. l. impr. by Cawood,
and 2 more

1055 Viret's expoſition in the apoſtles crede, bl. l. impr. - . 2. 6 *D.º*
by Day, and 3 more

1056 Becon's governaunce of vertue, b. l, impr. by Day, - . 3. 6 *D.*
1566. Northbrook's common places, bl. 1600.
Lambert upon the wyl of man, bl. l. by Day, 1548

1057 Calvin's catechiſme, bl. l. 1586, and 6 more - . 1. 6 *Tutet*

1058 The diſplaying the family of love, bl. l. impr. by _ 2. _ *WWhite.*
Middleton, 1579, and 3 more

1059 The world poſſeſſed with devils, viz. of the devil - . 6. _ *Mechee.*
let loose and the white and black devils, 1583,
a famous ſermon, &c. round hyd in a wall in 1388,
bl, l. impr. by Awdely, 1575

60 Bera's

1.6 1060 Beza's Piththie fumme of the chriſtian faith, bl. l. m. b. and 2 more

Tutet   _. 3. _ 1061 The obedience ɩf a chriſtian man, b. l. m. g. l. impr. by Coplande. Hughe's troubled man's medicine, bl. l. m. g. l. impr. by Jugge,   1548

B.White.   _. 4. _ 1062 Eraſmus's expoſycyon of the comune crede, b. l. m. g. l. impr. by Redman. hanſome weapon of a chriſtian hnight, neat impr. by Robt. Toy

Tutet.   _. 4.6 1063 A counter poyſon, modeſtly written for the time, b. l. m. g. l. printed by Waldgrave. Beza's markes of the Catholique churche, b. l. m. g. l. printed by Waldegrave

_. 7. _ 1064 Stubbes's anatomy of Abuſes, b. l. m. impr. by Jones, 1583. A pleaſaunt dialogue between a ſouldier of Barwicke, and an Engliſh chaplain, bl. l. m. g. . and 1 more

D?   _. 3. _ 1065 Bucer's reſolution concernyng the apparel of miniſters, &c. bl. l. m. g. l. A difcourſe againſt the outwarde apparell and miniſtring garmentes of the Popiſh church, m. g l.   1566

WE.   _. 6.6 1066 Admonitions to the parliament, b. l. m. g. l. The life off the 70th archbiſhop. bl. l. m g. l. 1574 Halbrydge's epiſtle exhortatorye of an Englyſhe chriſtiane, b. l. m. g. l.

Tutet   _. .3.6 1077 Jewel on the Theſſalonians, m. g. l. 1594. Gryneus on Haggeus the prophet, m. g. l.   1586

Bartlett.   _. 7. _ 1078 The terrible and helpleſſe burnying of Paules church in London, by lyghtnynge, b. l. m, g. l. impr. by Wylliam Seres   1561

_. 4.6 1079 Melanthon's apologie, that is to ſay, the Defence of the confeſcyon of the Germaynes, by Taverner, b. l. m. g. l. impr. by Redman   1536

D?   _. 8.6 1080 Apothegmes, quicke, wittie, and ſentencious ſayinges of philoſophiers, &c. b. l. tracſlated into Englyſhe by Udall, m. g. l. Lond. impr. by Kingſton   1564

Nicol.   _. 4.6 1081 Turbervile's herovcall epiſtles cf Oide, b. l. m. b. printed by Staffod, 1600, Sir Thomes More's pleaſaunt and wittie worke, called Uopia, b. l, impr. by Weale   1556

D?.   _. 9. 6 1082 A looking glaſſe for the court, tranſlated by Briant, b. l. 1575, ſeven curious ancient traĉts, b. l. impr. by Berthelet, Daye, &c. 1534, &c.

         1083 Joye

£. s. d
16. 6. 6

1083 Joye on the prophete Ifaye, b. l. m. g. l. printed in — .4. 6
Stratfbarg   1531
1084 The primer of Henry the 8th, b. l. m. g. l. impr. — . 6. 6 VWhite
by Thomas Potyt, 1542, the Pfalmes epitomized,
trasflated by Taverner, b. l. m. g. l. impr. 1539
1085 The heroical devices of Paradin, cuts, m. b. 1591 — . 11. — Nicol.
the alcoran of the barefote friers, b. l.   1550
1086 the breviary of Britagne tranfla ed by Twyne, bl. l. m. — . 9. — D.º
g. l. impr. by Jhones, 1573. the Perfian monarchic,
by Livelie, bl. l. m. g. l. printed by Kingfton, 1597
1087 Stow's fummarie of Englysfhe chronicles, a fair copy, — . 2. — Tutet
b. l. impr. br Marfhe   1565
1088 Beza's New Teftament, 1581. prayers and adminift. — . 2. 6 WF
of the Sacramentes   1584
1089 the Newe Teftament, b. l. very ancient imper. — . 5. 6 D.º
m. g. l.
1090 another copy, bl, l. by Coverdale, cuts, impt. m. b. — . 10. 6
antv.   1526
1091 Smythe's defence of the facrament of the aulter, b. l. — . 3. — Tutet
neat,   1546
1092 the new teffament, bl. l. wants title, c. m. g. l. — . 5. 6 Fox
1093 Hore beate Marie Virginis, a Mfr. on velium, cum — . 9. — B. White.
fig. 1437
1094 a very curious Mfs. on vellum, finely illuminated   — . 16. — Tutet
1095 Horæ, B. V. Mariæ, ad ufum romane curie, cum — . 17. —
fig.   1493
1096 devotions, in Englifh manufcript, on vellum   — . 11. — D.ºHunter
1097 a curious Mfs. bible on virgin vellum, finely illumi- 2. 10. — Mole.
nated, m. g. l.
1098 les amours paftorales de Daphnis and Chloe, avec. 1. 11. 6
fig. par Phillipus and audran, c. t. g. l.   1718.

QUARTO.

1099 The fecretes of Alexis of Piedmont, b. l. 1568. — . 7. —
Tuffer's 500 points of good hufbandry, bl. l. 1638.
Ciifford's fchoole of horfmanfhip, bl. l. 1585, and
3 more
1100 a tragedie or dialogue of the unjufte ufurped prima- — . 6. 6 WF.
cie of the bifhop of Rome, tranflated by Ponet, bl. l.
imperfect, 1549, and 10 more
1101 S owe's furvey of London, bl. l. 1618 and 3 more — . 3. —
1102 Hiftory of Palmerin of England, bl. l. impr. Lylie's — . 2. 6
eupheus and his England, bl. l. and one more
1103 Pope's

-. 4. - 1103 Pope's Homer's iliad, vol. 1ft aud 5th, 1715
-. 4. 6 1104 two old bl. letter Bibles, wants the titles
Mole   -. 10. -1105 pfalmodia Luneburgi, m. b. 1569, and 8 more
Chapman -. 3. 6 1106 hiftoi e de la vie de David, avec fig. Paris. 12 pri-
morum Cæfarum, per Hulfium, cum fig, fpiræ typis,
B. Albini   1599
Fox   -. 2. - 1107 illuft ium virorum epiftolæ, a Sylvio, and 7 more
WF.   -. 3. 6 1108 Salluft i opera, Paris, 1544, Dares Phrigius, cum fig.
Pariffis, a Gaudoul, and one more
-. 6.6 1109 textus Alexandri cum fententiis & conftructionibus,
impr. Martini Antv. 1493. Cathalogus illuftrium
virorum Germaniæ, 1495. Scribendi orandi. modus, per Ant. Mancinellum, Venet.   1493
-. //. - 1110 difcours de l'origine des armes, avec fig. 1658, and
5 more
Mann. -. 4. - 1111 cor. Agrippæ de occulta philofophia lib. tres, Antv.
1531. Alchemiæ gebri Arabis philofophi, nuremb.
1545. Hippocratis de morbis   Paris 1540
-. 6.6 1112 Stow's chronicles, bl. l. 1590. An abridgment cf
Grafton's chronicle, bl. l.   1557
-. 5. 6 1113 hyftory of two noble captaynes of the world, Annibal
and Scipio, bl. l. m. b.   1590
Mann -. 3. 6 1114 Cattan's geomancie, with cuts, bl. l. Lond. printed
by Wolfe   1591
Dr. Chauncey .8. - 1115 Fortefcue's forefte or collection of hiftories lefs profitable than pleafant, b. l. m. b. impr. by Kingfton
1571
-. /4. - 1116 Hill's fountaine of fame, erected in an orcharde of
amorous adventures, b. l. m. g. l. impr. by Charle-
wood   1580
Mole   -. 6. -1117 Harveys defence of Brutes and the Brutans hiftory,
b. l. m. g. l. impr. by Wolfe   1593
Tutet   -. 3. - 1118 Huartes's examination of men's wits, m. g. l. Lond.
by Iflip   1594
Gray   - . 4. - 1119 a thoufaud notable things of fundrie thoughts, b. l.
m. g. l.   1595
Tutet   -. 5. -1120 Hill's fchoole of fkil, bl. m. g. l. Lond. printed by
Judfon,   1599
Nicol   -. 5.6 1121 the lawier's logicke, by Fraunce, b. l. m. g. l. imprt
by How   1588
Tutot.   - . 6.6 1122 Lluyd's pilgrimage of prlnces, b. l. m. g. l. printed
by Jones

£. s. d
29. 16. 6.

1123 Lavatelus of ghostes and spirites walking by nyght, — .15. — Mole
and of straunge noyses, crackes, &c. before mens
death, b. l. m. g. l. a fine copy, printed by Bynneman   1572
1124 Afcham's fchoolmafter, b. l. m. g. l.   1589 — .5. — Brander
1125 Morwyng's treafure of Evonymus the wonderful hid — .10. — D:
fecretes of nature, cuts, b. l. m, g. l. by Daie 1559
1126 Agrippa's vanitie of arts and fciences, b, l, m, b, — .2. 6 Cozens
imprinted by Bynneman   1575
1127 Twyne's phificke againft fortune, b, l, m, b, Lond, — .7. 6
Watkyns   1579 Connaught
1128 Whetftone's Englifh mirror, b, l, m, g, l, Windet, — .8. 6 Nicol
1586
1129 Pierce Penileffe his fupplication to the divell, b, l, — .5. 6 Mechee
m, b. Jeffes   1592
1130 the inftitution of a chriften man, b, l, m, g, l, Berr — .5. — Cozens.
thelet   1537
1131 De la Now's politique and militarie difcourfes, b, l, — .2. —
m, b, Orwin   1587 Connaught
1132 Boffewell's workes of armorie, b, l, Tottell, 1572, — .7. 6 Tutet
accidens of armorie, cuts, coloured, Tottell 1576
1133 Ferne's blazon of gentrie, cuts, m, g, l, London, — .17. 6 Williams
Windet   1586
1134 the rule of reafon, contayning the arte of logicke, by — .6. 6 Nicol.
Wilfon, impr. Kingfton, 1567, the art of rhetor-
icke Englifhed by Wilfon, b, l, m, b, Robinfon,
1585
1135 arte of navigation, cuts, tranflated by Eden, b, l, — .2. 6 WH
m, b, Jugge   1572
1136 Mafterfon's booke of arithmeticke, m, g, l, Field, — 3. — Cozens.
1592
1137 the booke of Lucarfolace devifed by Lucar, 6 t. g, l, — .1. 6
Field.   1592
1138 arte of limming, paynting, &c. b, l, fewed, Purfoote, — .6. Brander
1583, Italian banquet, fhewing the manner how to
dreffe flefh, foules, or fifhes, &c. b, l, fewed 1578
1139 Vowell's offices of the citie of Excefter, b, l, a cata- — .9. 6 Nicol.
log of the bifhops of Excefter, m, b, Denham, 1584,
a proclamation for the obfervation of certaine ftatutes, b, l, m, b, 1562 and 4 of Elizabet
1140 Smyth de republica Anglorum in Englyfhe, b, l, m, — .10. 6
b. Middleton 1583, the commonwealth and govern-
ment of Venice, by Lewkenor, neat, London, 1599
1141 Arceus's method of curing wounds in the head, &c. — 3. —
b. l. m. b. Eaft   1588

H

£. s. d
36. 14. 6

Branding —. 3.6 1142 Elyot's caftle of helth, b, l, m, b, Berthelet 1541
D° —. 2.— 1143 Paynell's regiment of health, b, l, m, b, T. Creede, 1597
D° —. 4.—. 1144 Cogan's haven of health, b, l. m, b. Field 1596
Mole —. 5.— 1145 a worke for the prefervation of helth, tranflated by L M, m, g, l,, Wolfe 1588
Brandj —. 2.— 1146 Clever's flower of phificke, b, l, m, g, l, Ward 1590
D° —. 4.6 1147 Boorde's breviary of health, b, l, m, b, Powell 1557
Fox. —. 2.6 1148 Blower's ftore houfe or treafury for the difeafed, b, l, m, g, l, Purfoot 1596
—. 6.— 1149 the booke of diftillations by Baker, with cuts, b, l. m, g, l, Denham 1576
Brandj —. 3.6 1150 Coffike's whetftone of witte, arithmetike, &c, b, l, m, b, Kingfton 1557
D° —. 7.6 1151 cyvile and uhcyvile life, very profitable and pleafant to read, b, l, m, g, l, Jones, 1574, the honourable reputation of a fouldier, wants title, b, l, m, b, by Whetftone
D° —. 11.6 1152 the images of the Old Teftament, bound in vellum, Lyons, 1549
Thane 1.12.— 1153 here begyuneth, the life of Robert the Devyll, a poem, in MS with curious cuts
B. White. —. 6.— 1154 Alexis's 680 fecrets in phyfic and furgerie, b. l. m. g. l. impr. by Denham, 1569
—. 2.6 1155 a moft excellent hyftorie of princes and kingdoms, b. l. impr. by Bynneman, 1571, More's ftate of Utopia, b l. Lond. prin. by T. Creede, 1597
Brandr 1.8.6 1156 Fitzherbert's expofi of the king's prerogative, by —. 2.6 Hamforde, b. l. m. g. l. impr by Tottle, 1573
Nicol. 1.8.6 1157 the boke of the cyte of ladyes, b. l. m. b. cuts, impr. by Pepwell, 1521
Brandj —. 8.— 1158 the primer of King Henry the VIIIth, b. l. m. b. impr. by Witchurche, 1545
—. 4.6 1159 the Newe Teftament, b. l. m. g. l. impr. by Jugge, *With the Old Teft.* 1569
Mole —. 4.6 1160 ———— ———— very neat, printed at Rhemes, by John Fogny, 1582
Brandj —. 12.— 1161 hore beatiffime virgins Marie, ad Sarifburienfis, cum fig. b. l. c. t. g. l. Lond. 1537
Nicol. —. 5.— 1162 the firft white letter and dip thongues, by Pynfon, 1509, fermo hieronymi de navitates domin, printed by Pynfon, 1509, the lyfe of the gloryous vyrgyn faynt Barbara, b. l. printed by Julyn Notari, 1518, the lyfe of St. Erafmus, b. l. by Julyn Notary, 1520

£. s. d
44. 14 6

1163 the booke of honor and armes, cuts, m b. printed, - .12. _ *Williams*
by Richard Jhones, 1590, Norden's mirrour of
honor, *m. b.* Lond. printed by the Widowe Orwin,
1597

1164 fcala Perfectionis, *b. l.* Lond. imp by Julian Notary - *11. 6 E.*
1507

1165 linacri rudimento grammatices, Lat. and Eng. m. - .4. _
g l. Londini, per Pynfon

1166 Libellus de Confcribendis epiftolis, authore D'Eraf- - .13. _ *Nicol.*
mo, *m. b.* Cantab, 1521

1167 Poftillas five Expofitiones epyft. & evang. *b. l.* Lon- - .4. _ *Brand*
dini Juliani Notarii, 1500

1168 the primer, printed on vellum, and bound in ditto *1. 4.* _ *Macarty.*
Purchased by Ratcliff of Herbert 1535

1169 a very curious Latin MSS. on vellum, which treats _ .12.6 *Brandj*
of the caufes and relative effects of difeafes, the
manner of adorning women, N. B. vide 12 leaf,

1170 a very curious Latin Bible, inprefia venetiis per de - .13.6 *Knight.*
Bailbrun, 1483

1171 l'hiftoire & plaifante cronique du noble and vaillant _ .2. _
Baudouyn Conte de Flandres lequell efpoufale le
Dyable, avec fig. colorees

1172 Cooper's chronicle, b. l. Lond. prin. by Marfhe, - *6.* _ *Brandj.*
1559

1173 an epitome of Froflard's chronicle, by Golding, _ .6. _ *Thane.*
1608, and 4 other tracts

1174 fafciculus temporum omnes antiquornm cronicas fuc- _ .5. _ *Brandj.*
cincte completens, cum fig b. l. m. b. Paris, 1518

F O L I O.

1175 Fuller's hiftory of the holy warre 1647, and 4 more - .3.

1176 Auftin's meditations (with his portrait, by Glover) _ .5. _ *Fox*
1633, and 2 more

1177 Vigon's chirurgery, b. l. impr. by Whytchurch, _ .4.6 *D?*
1543, Diggs's pantometria, 1591, and 2 more

1178 Bentivolio and Urania, by Ingelo, Killegrew's - .5.6
plays, fewed, 1663

1179 Livy's roman hiftory, by Holland, Plutarch's lives by _ .8. _ *Mann.*
North

1180 les œuvres de Virgille, avce fig. Paris, 1551 - .8. _ *Cater*

1181 le neufiefme livre d'amudis de Gaule, Paris, 1551 _ .4.6

1182 ftate tracts in K. William's time, 2 v. ditto in _ .7.6 *D?*
Charles the IId's time

1183 Ovidi epiftolæ, cum comment. 1529, Horatii opera, _ .4.6 *Brandj.*
ap. Alcenlium, 1519

L. s. d
54. 0. —

*1. 5. — *1184 les croniques d'enguerran, de Monſtrelet, 3 tom.
Paris, 1572

F. —.7.6 1185 Fox's book of martyrs, imperfeɕt, b. l impr. by
Day, 1563 (with the portrait of the printer

—.4. — 1186 Matt. Paris hiſtoria Angliæ, Lond. 1571, Scapulæ
lexicon, Baſil

Brand. —.5.6 1187 Sleidan's commentaries, b. l. impr. by Daye, 1560,
Calvin's inſtitutes, b. l.   1561

Chapman. —.4. — 1188 Hieronymi opera, 1508, ſermones dominicales Hu-
gonis de Prato, very old but no date

—.4.6 1189 a volume containing 85 miſcellaneous traɕts (with
the portrait of Jacobus Sharpe, arch bp. of St Andrews)   1661

—,5. — 1190 Grafton's chronicle, b. l. three leaves wanting, 1568

—.10. — 1191 Fox's book of martyrs, 2 v. b. l. impr. by Daye,
1683

D. Gifford —.8. — 1192 Eraſmus's paraphraſe on the Newe Teſt. 2 v. b. l.
printed by Whitchurch,   1548

Thane —.6. — 1193 miſſale ad vſum ecclef. Saliſburinſis, Paris, per Regnault,   1529

D? —.2. — 1194 regiſtrum omnium brevium oⅰiginalium, per Wm.
Raſtell,   1531

Macarty —.7.6 1195 compendium errorum Johannis Pape, 22, a Guil.
Okam,   1583

B White —.10.6 1196 Hortus ſanitatis, de herbis et plantis, b. l. colorat

D? 1.16. — 1197 Ænec Silvii epiſtolæ, Lovaniæ, Joane de Weſtfalia,
1483

Williams —.19. — 1198 a manuſcript on heraldry, coloured

Thane 2.16. — 1199 Hardyng's chronicle, in verſe, a mſs. very ancient

Macarty —.9. — 1200 Alberti magni de phiſico libri oɕto. Venetiis 1494

Thane 1.2. — 1201 Ludolphi meditationes de vitæ Jeſu Chriſti, b.l, m,
g. l, ſine anno

—.7. — 1202 las quatro partes enteras de la cronicv de Eſpana, per
Don Alonſo, el ſabio, one leaf wrote, a curious
and ſcarce book ———   1541

D. Hunter —.16. — 1203 Robarte of Gloceſter his chronicle, in mſs, this Robert lived about the end of King Henry III.

D? —.8. — 1204 Guido bonatus traɕtatus aſtronomie, b. l, cum fig. m,
g. l,   —   Venet. 1506

Thane 1.15. — 1205 Samuelis ſcrutinium ſcripturarum, b. l, m, g. l.
Mantua 1475

Brand —.7.6 1206 intrationum lib. omnibus legitus hominibus, b. l, m,
g. l, Pynſon ———   1510

Edwards —.7. — 1207 the works of Geffray Chauce, by Thynn, b. l,
printed by Godfrey   1532

Brader. —.8.6 1208 Hanmer's ancient eccleſiaſtical hiſtories, b. l, m, g l,

£. s. d
69. 0. 6

imp. by Vautrollier   1585
1209 Dodoens, new herball, or hiftorie of plantes, neat, b. — . 8 . —
      l, printed by Dewes   1578
1210 Guevera's dial of princes, b. l, very neat, Englyfh'd — . 5 . 6
      by North, imp. by Tottill and Marfhe,   1568
1211 Bartholomeus de proprietatibus rerum, b. l, by Ber- — .13 . —
      thelet, 1535
1212 another coyp ditto, g. l, b. l, imp. by Wynkyn de 1. 8. —
      Worde
1213 Æfop's fables, b, l, cuts, impr. by Pynfon   1.16 . —
1214 Virgyle's Eneydos, b. l. 5 leaves, wrote, m, g, l, by 2 . 5 . —
      Caxton   1490   Durant
1515 the bok of fame, made by Gefferey Châucer, b, l, 3. 12. —
      m, g, l, by ditto, no date   B White.
1216 hiftorie of Charles the Grete, b, l, m, b, 1485, by 4. 4. —
      ditto
1217 the dyctes and notable wyfe fayenges of the philo- 15. 15
      fophers, b, l, m, g, l, by ditto   1477   Willet
1218 the lyfe of our lady, b, l, m, g, l, impr. by Caxton, 4 .4 . —
      no date   Dr. Hunter
1219 lyf of Saint Katherin of Senis, the blefled Virgin, 3. 3
      b, l, m, g, l, by Caxton, no date   Nical
1220 the book of the pylgremage of the fowle, b, l, m, b, 3. 17. —
      by Caxton   1483
1221 ——— of the fayt of Armes and of Chyvalrye, b, l, 3. 10. —
      m, g, l, by ditto   1489   White.
1222 the mirrour of the world, or thymage of the fame, 8. 10. —
      b, l, m, g, l, by ditto   1480   B. White
1223 — hiftory, of Reynart the foxe, b, l, m, g, l, by 6. 16. 6
      ditto   1481   Nicol.
1224 — boke intituled Eracles, and alfo of Godefrey of 4. — . —
      Boloyne b, l, m, g, l, by Caxton   1481   D?
1225 Gower de confeffione Amantis, b, l, m, g, l, by 5. 10. —
      Caxton   1483   D°
1226 Chaucer's workes, the firft edit. b, l, m, g, l, fuppo- 6. — . —
      fed to be printed about 1476, by Caxton   Shropfhire
1227 the boke called the mirrout of the world, a MS. on — .13. —
      vellum   Dr. Hunter.
1228 the bokys of haukyng and hnntyng, with other 9. 12. —
      plefuris dyverfe as in the boke apperis, and alfo of
      coot-armuris, a nobull worke, b, l, cuts coloured,   Shropfhire
      m, g, l, printed at St. Albones   1486
1229 the holy Bible, with Beza's notes, maps and cuts, 2. 10. —
      Turkey, ruled, Lond.   1708   Mole

        End of the Seventh Day's Sale.

                                       £ 150. 0. 6

Eighth Day's Sale,

THURSDAY, APRIL 4, 1776.

l. s. d

OCTAVO & DUODECIMO.

Rogers -. *6.* - 1230 MILLS on the management of bees, and 9 more, few'd

*Hallam*_. *6.* - 1231 three bundles of pamphlets, law, fermons, on the Trinity, &c.

Conna.—. *2. 6* 1232 Ames's catalogue of Englifh heads   1748

A   -. *1. 6* 1233 Barrow's fermons, and 11 more

Collins -. *7.* - 1234 the pfalmes, in 4 languages, holy Bible, v. 2d and

B   */.*   3d, imp by Day, and 5 more

D.°   _. *2. 6* 1235 confolatorium timorate confcientie, per Ryder, b. l, m, g. l, vita patris Benedicti, a D. Gregorio, mag. Gr. & Lat, nitid, 1602, and 2 more

Tutet _. *2. 6* 1236 Eufebii hiftoria ecclefiaftica, b. l, Paris, a Regaault, and 5 more

   _. *2. 6* 1237 Banks's hiftory of Germany, 1763, and 2 more

Nicol. - *7. 6* 1238 a collection of fcarce, choice and valuable tracts, not to be found but in the libraries of the curious, 1721

Hallam _. *1. 6* 1239 Williams's fermons, 2 v, and 2 more

2 D.°   _. *7. 6* 1240 a collection of mfs. fermons, by the Rev. Mr. Ratcliffe, preached about the year, 1720 to 1727

Tutet _. *4. 6* 1241 the garden of wyfdome, by Taverner, b. l, m. b, imp. by Copland, caftle of memorie, by Fulwood, b. l, m. b, printed by Hall   1562

Wh. _. *8.* - 1242 the clofet of counfells, by Elviden, b. l, m. b, imp. by Colwell, 1569, a lyttell treatyfe in verfe. to the Cardinall of Yorke dedicate, rede me and be not wrothe, for I faye no thynge but trothe; b. l, m. b.

£. s. d
2.19. 6

1243 an introduction to the love of God, by Fletcher, b. 1, – .3 _ *Davis*
m. b, imp. by Parfoote, 1581, a warning againſt
papiſtes, by Norton, b. l, m. b, imp. by John
Daye

1244 Wicklieffe's wicket, b. l, m, g. l, Beza's lyfe and – .8. 6 *Do*
death of Calvin, b. l, c. t, g, l. imp. by Denham,
1564

1245 ane detectioun of the duinges of Marie Quene of – .11. 6 *Nicol.*
Scottes touchand the murder of hir huſband, and hir
conſpiracie, adulterie and pretenſed mariage with
the Erle Bothwell, tranſlated by G. B. b. l, m,
g. l, a fine copy and very ſcarce, imp. at Edinb-
1568

1246 the boke of huſbandry, b l, m, g. l, imp by Ber– – 10. 6
thelet,, the boke of ſurveyinge, b. l, m, g. l, imp.
by Berthelet

1247 the cronycle of Sir John Oldecaſtell, by Bale, with – .6. 6 *Do*
his portrait, b. l, neat. imp. by Scoloker, the tragical death of David Beaton, biſhop of St. An-
drewes, in Scotland, b. l, m, g. l, imp. by Daye

1248 the boke of nobilitye, by Humphrey, b. l, neat, – 11. _ *D*
imp. by Marſhe, 1563, the inſtitucion of a gentleman, b l, m, g. l, imp. by Marſhe   1553

1249 the confeſſyon of the fayth of the Germaynes, by Ta– – .5. _ *Rogers*
verner, b. l, m, g. l, imp. by Redman   1536

1250 a ſhort cronycle of the kings of England, mayers and – .3. _ *BWhite*
ſheriffes of the citie of London, m, g. l, imp. by
Byddell, Stowe's chronicles of England, Scotland
imperf. b. l, m, g. l, 1560, and 1 more

1251 conſtitutions provincialles of Otho and Octhobone, – .9. _ *Nicol.*
b. l, m, g. l, imp by Redman, 1534, the account
of the Spaniſh Armado, againſt England, b. l, m,
g. l, imp. by Wolfe   1583

1252 the keye of philoſophie, by Heſter, b. l, m. b, printed – .6. _ *WH.*
by Richard Day, 1580, the boke of meaſuryng of
Lande, by Sir Richard de Boneſe, b. l, m. imp. by
Colwell, and one more

1253 the difference betwene the auncient phiſicke, againſt – .6. 6 *Bartlet*
Gallen, &c. b. l, m, g. l, imp. by Weley, 1585, a
confutation of aſtrologie, by Heth, b. l, m b,
prin ed by Waldegrave   1583

1254 a greene foreſt, or a natural hiſtorie of ſtones, met- *1. 1. Do*
tals, herbes, plantes, ſhruos, beaſtes, fowles, fiſhes,
&c by Maplet, b. l, imp. by H l enham, 1567, the
compoſt of Ptholomeus, prince of aſtronomye, b. l,
m, g. l, imp. by Wyer

£. s. d

8. 1. –

–. 2. 6 1255 the Frenche Littleton, or French grammar, by Hol-
lyband, m, g. l, imp. by Vautrolliere the Latine
grammar of P. Ramus, tranflated into Englifh, 1585,

.–. 7. 6 1256 the burnynge of Bucer and Phagius at Cambrydge in
the tyme of Quene Mary. b. l, m g. l, imp. by
Marfhe, 1562, the ephemerides of Phialo, by Goffon, b. l, m. b, imp. by Dawfon   1586

–. 4. – 1257 Arcandam of phyfiognomy, very pleafant to read, b.
l, imp. by Marfhe, 1578, the Ethiques of Ariftotle,
b. l, m. b. imp. by Grafton, 1547, perpetual prog-
noftications of the change of weather, b, l, m. b,
1578

–. 6. – 1258 a direction for the health of magiftrates and ftudents,
by Newton, b. l, m. b, 1574, the regiment of health,
by Paynell, b. l, m b, imp. by Howe   1575

–. 2. 6 1259 a compendium of rationall fecrets of Phioravante, b.
l, m b, imp. by Kingfton, 1582, a dialogue bothe
pleafant and pityfull, againft the peftilence, &c. b.
l. by Builein. m. b, imp. by Kingfton   1578

–. 17. – 1260 the ftratagemes, flaughters and policies of Julius
Frontinus, tranflated by Moryfme, b. l, m, g. l.
imp. by Berthelet, 1532, Ono fandro Platonico, of
the generall captaine, and of his office, englyfh'd by
Whytehorne. b. l, m, g. l, imp. by Seres   1563

–. 6. 6 1261 hore beati virginis, cum fig. fine tit. b. l, m, b. the
helluyfhe Spanifhe inquifition, in Dutch, m, g. l,
by Daye ——   1569

–. 11. 6 1262 the pleafante and wittie playe of the cheafts, by
Rowbothum, b. l, m, g. l, printed by Hall, 1562,
the arte or crafte of rhetoryke, by Cox, b. l, m, g.
l, imp. by Redman

–. 6. – 1263 the arte of chiromancy and phifiognomy, tranflated
by Withers, b. l, m, g. l, by Day, 1558, the arte
of reafon rightly termed witcraft, by Lever, b. l,
m, g. l, imp. by Bynneman   1573

–. 4. 6 1264 the inftitution of a chirurgion, compiled by Gale, b.
l, neat, printed by Hall   1573

1. 5. – 1265 the newe teftament, b, l. neat, imp, at Antwerp, by
Martin Emperoue   1534

1. 4. – 1266 another copy, by Tindall, b, l, cuts, a fine copy, m,
g, l,   1534

–. 11. – 1267 the byrth of Mankynde, named the womans booke,
cuts, by Reynold, b. l. m. g. l. imp. by Ray 1545

1268 the gofpell of St. Marke, and 2 more MSS. on vellum

– 2. 6 1269 a curious manufcript, in a cafe

£ s d
15.2.6

1270 lingua. or fhe combat of the tongue, and the five —.7. — DʳHunter.
   fenfes for the fuperiority, a pleafant comadie, printed by Okes, 1617, Daniel his Chaldie vifions and
   his ebrew, with cuts, printed by Field, 1596, and
   4 more
1271 bibliotheca philofophorum clafficorum author, — .5. 6
   chronologica, a Frifio, 1592, and 5 more
1272 Bilfon's fermons, at Paules Croffe, b, l, 1599, and 3 _ .1. 6
   more
1273 Smith's common wealth of England, 1609, the con- _ .10. 6
   quefte of the Weft India, and 4 more, b, l,
1274 the moft ftrange and admirable difcoverie of the 3 _ .8.
   witches of Warboys, b, l, 1593, Lyiit's euphues,
   the anatomie of wit, b, l, 1636 and 4 more
1275 painter's palace of pleafure, 3 v. b, l, imperfeft   — .12. —
1276 Latymer's fermons, and 15 more, b, l, .before 1600 _ .10. 6
   imperfect
1277 31 volumes, bound and unbound, for and againft the — .9. 6
   Puritans
1278 Arbuthnot's tables of ancient coins, weights and — .14. —
   meafures, boards   1727
1279 de falfa & vera unius dei patris, filii & fpiritus fanfti, — .11. —
   m, g, l, I principi fanti con, of fervationi politiche
   de Rannuccio Pico di Parma, Palma, m, g, l, 1622
1280 Effai philofophique concernant l'entendament hu- — .4. 6
   main, par Locke, m, g, l, 1729 Le Sage Encour
   de Matt Peregrini, m, g, l,   Paris 1638
1281 Pappe with an hatchet, alias, a figge for my god- 1. 4. —
   foone, or cracke me this not, writen by one who
   dares call a dog a dog and made to prevent Martin's
   dog duies, impr. by John Anoke and John Aftile,
   an almond for a parrat, or Cutbert curry knaves
   almes; fit for the knave Martin and the reft of the
   impudent beggars, with 4 more equally humorous
1282 the vifion of Pierce Plowman, b, l, m, b, imp, by — .15. — Bartlet
   Rogers, 1561, Pierce the plowman's crede, b, l,
   m, b,   R. Wolfe .1553.
1283 Gifford's pofie of gilloflowers, b, l, m, b, imp, by — .16. 6
   Perin, 1580, Willobie his Avifa, or a true picture
   of a maid, m, b, impr. by Winiet, 1594, Watfon's
   paffionate centurie of love, b, l, m, b, imp, by
   Wolfe
1284 the vifion of Pierce Plowman, b, l, m, b, g, l, imp, — 8. 6
   by Crowley   1550

I

—. 4.6. 1285. Langham's garden of health, b, l, m, g, l, Lᵐ
     impr,   15

Bartlett —. 7. — 1286 Baker's practice of. phificke, b, l, m, g, l, prin, by
     Short,   1599

1.1. — 1287 the courte of civill courtefie, b, l. m, b. imp, by
     Jhones 1577, the hve way to the Spyttell Houfe,
     b, l, neat, hy Copland, Hyke Scorner, b, l, neat,
     printed by Waley

White —. 1.6 1288 confpiracie for pretended reformation, m, b, 1592
     Gyffard's reply to Greenwood and 1 more

D° —. 2. 6 1289 Sutcliffe's treatife of ecclefiaftical defcipline, m, b,
     1591 and 3 more

D° —. 1.6 1290 Belfon's perpetual government of the church, m, b,
     imp, by Daye,   1547

— . 7. 6 1291 Cope's meditacion upon feleft pfalmes, b, l, m, b,
     imp, by Daye, 1547, injunctions gyven by the
     Bp, of Salifbury through his dioces, b, l, m,

Tidet —. 7. — 1292 ecclefiaftical deience againft dges, m, g, l, 1588,
     and two more

Cozens. —. 5. 6 r293 the examinations of Barrowe, Grenewood and Penrie,
     b, l, m, g, l, 1589, Greenwood's anfwer to Gifford,
     m, l, m, g, l,   1590

— . 3. — 1294 examinations of Barrowe, &c. Barrowe's refutation
     of Giffard, Penry's reformation, no enemy to the
     ftate, m, g, l,   1590

—. 10. 6 1295 Cranmer's defence of the facrament, b, l, m, g, l,
     impr. by Wolfe, 1550, a neceffrry doctrine and eru-
     dition for any chriften man, b, l, m, g, l, impr. by
     Berthelet   1543

— . 2. 6 1296 Marbecke's lives of the holy fainctes, prophetes, &c.
     b, l,   1574

Thane — . 9. — 1297 the homilies of King Edward VI. b, l, 1550

—. 12. — 1298 the primer of King Henry VIII. b, l, neat, Lat and
     Englifh   1545

Connaught —. 8. 6 1299 Cooper's expofition of the old teftament as redde in
     the church at common prayer on Sondayes, b, l, m,
     g, l, impr. by Denham   1573

Nicol. — . 10. 6 1300 Higins's mirrour for magiftrates, b, l, m, g, l, impr.
     by Hen. Marlhe   1587

WH. — . 4. 6 1301 Becon's new poftil, containing fermons upon the
     Sonday gofpelles, b, l, m, g, l, impr. by Marfhe,
     1560

Davis — . 7. — 1302 Bale's ymage of both churches, b, l, m, g, l, impr.
     by Wver   1556

Dr Chauncy — . 17. — 1303 —— pageant of popes, b, l, m, g, l, 1574

E. — . 10. — 1304 Tuffer's 500 pointes of good hufbandrie, b, l, m,
     g, l, prin. by Denham   1586

L. s. d
30. 7. -

1305 The Eneydos of Virgil, by Phaer, b, l, m, g, l - .9. - *Nicol.*
prin, by Hall   1562
1306 another copy in 13 books, b, l, by Twyne, m, g, - .11. - *D'Hunt*
l, prin, by Creede   1596
1307 Ferton's fecrete wonders of nature, b, l, m, g, l, - .15.6 *Gray*
impr. by Bynneman   1569
1308 Gafcoigne's works, that is to fay, his flowers, - .17 *F.*
herbes &c, &c, b, l, m, b, impr, by Jeffes 1587
1309 a book of chriftian prayers, in Queen Elizabeth's - .16. - *Cater.*
time, cuts b, l, m, g, l, prin, by Yardley 1590
1310 the Pedegrewe of Heretiques, with a curious cut, - .8. - *Cozens.*
b, l, m, g. l, impr, by Denham   1566
1311 Saint. Peter's complaint; Saint Peter's path to the - .6. - *D*.º
joys of heaven, the betraying of Chrift, Judas in
difpaire, b, l, m, g, l,   1598
1312 the troubles of Franckford in Germany, in 1554 - .3. - *Thane*
aboute the book of common prayer, b, l, m g l,
1576
1313 Barnes's fupplication to King Henry 8th b, l, m g, - .3. - *Cozens*
imp, by Bydell   1534
1314 a full and plain declaration of ecclefiaftical difci- - .3. - *Nicol*
pline, b, l, m, g, l, 1574, Bp. Gardiner's declara-
tion againft George Joye, b, l, m, b,   1546
1315 Horace's arte of poetrie, piftles and fatyres, by- .16. -
Drant, b. l, neat, impr. by T. Marfhe   1567
1316 a treatife of the miniftery of the church of England, - .4.6
b, l, m, g, l, Nowell's catechifme, b, l, m, g, l,
prin. by J. Daye   1573
1317 the canticles or balades of Salomon, by Baldwin, b, - .8.6
l, m, g, l,   1549
1318 Howell his devifes for his own exercife and his 1.9. - *Reed*
friends pleafure, b, l, c, t, g, l, impr. by Jackfon,
1581, the prayfe of all women, b, l, m, g, l, impr.
&y Myddylton
1319 the golden aphroditis, by John Grange, gent. b, l, - .5.6 *BWhite*
m, b, Lond. 1577, the graund amour, b. l, m. b.
impr. by Waylande   1554
1320 Warner's Albion's England, b, l, m, g, l, impr by- .14. - *Thane*
Robinfon, 1586, the funeralles of Edward VIth,
with his portrait, imp. by Marfhe,   1536
1321 the fhepardes calander, b, l, cuts, m, g, l, prin. by 1. 2. - *Mafon*
Singleton, 1579, Whetfton's pieces, viz. the caftle
of delight, &c b, l, m, b, impr by Waley, 1576
1322 the fhepherdes calender, b, l, m, g, l, cuts, prin. by- .10. - *Mecham.*
Creede,   1975

L. s d.
40. 8. 6. 5.

White — .3. 1323 Hooper's confeffion and proteftation of the chriftian faythe, b, l, m, b, impr. by Daye, 1550, the apolo⁻ gie of the church of Englande, b, l, m. g. l. by Wolfe 1562

Connaught .8. 6 1324 Higgins's mirrour for magiftrates, b. l. very neat, imp, by Marſh 1575

— . 3. 6 1325 Vicary's anatomie of man's bodie, b. l. m. b. the zodiake of life tranflated by Googe, b, l. m, b. imp. by Robinfon 1588

Mafon — .9. — 1326 Phillis and Flora, 1598, the tragedie of Soliman and Perfeda, hypnerotomachia, or the ftrife of love in a dreame, with cuts, 1592

WI. — .1. — 1327 a true confiffion of the faith falfely called Browniſts, b. l. 1596, and 5 more, pamphlets for and againſt the puritans

Thane — . 8. — 1328 the Englifh Romayne lyfe, the lives of the Englifhmen at Rome, b. l. with 2 curious cuts, 1590, Martin's reconciliation of the clergy of England. b. l. printed by Windet 1590

D. — .1 6 1329 politique difcourfes tranflated by Radcliffe, 1578, Whitgiftes dangerous pofitions, imp. by Wolfe, 1593, and 1 more

Cater — .5. 6 1330 Cartwright's three books againſt Whitgifte, b. l. m. g. l. 1575

D: Hunter . 2. — 1331 an expofition upon St. John, by Marlorate, b. l. 1574 a parte of a regifter containing fundrie memorable matters, very fcarce, printed at Edinb. 1593

Collins — . 5. — 1332 Frampton's joyful newes out of the new found world, b. l. 1577, Higgins's mirour for magiſtrates, b. l. part the laſt 1574

Cater. — . 5. 6 1333 Dodoen's hiftorie of plants, b. l. 1586, the fecretes of Alexis of Piedmont, b. l. neat Pryn. by Hall 1562

Chapman. — . 12. 6 1334 hiftories of the wonderful fecretes in nature, cuts, b. l. imprinted by Bynneman, 1569, Vigo's chirurgerie, b. l. printed by Eaft, 1586, and two more

Reed — . 1. 6 1335 hiftory of the civil warres in France, b. l. by Colynet, 1598. the tragical hiftorie of the civil warres of the Low Countries, b. l. 1581

Dalby — . 5. — 1336 a quippe for an upftart courtier, b. l. a tragedie, or dialogue of the unjufte ufurp'd primacie of Bp. of Rome, tranflated by Ponét 1549

— . 2. — 1337 a fhort yet found commentarie on the Proverbs of Salomon b. l m. g. l. printed by Orwin

Thame — . 3. — 1338 the homilies of king Edward VIth. b. l. neat 1547

Nicol. — . 16. — 1339 an abridgement of the year books, b. l. m. g. l. by Pynfon

1340 Gemma Phrygius de principiis aftronomiæ et cofmo- _ _ 3. _ *Wood*
graphicæ, Jó. Grapheus typis, anno 1530, and 5
more

1341 Seneca de quatuor virtutibus cardinalibus, m. b. - - 9 _ *Thane*
1497, finonimorum Ciceronis, nit. imp. Pad. 1482 - .

1342 Plauti comœdiæ, nitid. g. l. Venet. 1495 — 6. _ *Catir*

1343 Lombardica hyftoria, m. b. g l. Bafil. 1490 _ 3. 6 *Macarty*

1344 vita et proceffus fancti Thome Cantuarienfis martyris _ 8. _ *Mason*
fuper libertate ecclefiaftica, nitid. g, l. Parif. 1495

1345 Jo. Nider confolatorium timoiatæ confcientiæ, m. g. 1. 16. _
l. Paris, 1478

1346 regimen fanitatis mediolenfis, g. l. impr. per Gering _ 16 *D.Hunter*
Paris, 1483

1347 Poftilla Nicolai de Lyra, fuper pfalterium, m. g. l. 1. 1. _ *Macarty*.
impr. per Gering, Paris, 1480

1348 exempla facre fcripture ex Veteri et Novo Teft. m. 2. 2. _
(liber rariffimus) Paris, 1477

1349 oratoria artis epitomata ars memoriæ, cum fig. (bib- 1. 1. _ *D.Hunter*
liotheca Colberlina, m. g. l Florent. 1482

1350 fynonoma magilli Jo. de Galendia, cum expofitione _ 4. 0 *Thane*
Galfiri di Anglici, m. b. Antv. 1492

1351 incipit Cordiale de quatuor noviffimis, de contemptu - 9. _ *Dampier*
mundi, &c. m. b. 1483

1352 le livre des trois filz des rois, et primierment com- _ 8. _ *Gough*
mente dieu au roy et a la royne, &c. avec fig. m. g.
l. impr. a Paris,

1353 Salamonis et Marcolphidyalogus, cum fig. Antv. - 6. _ *Thane*
per Gerardum, de Leau

1354 liber qui vocatir fpeculum chriftiani, impreff. Mach- 1. 4. _ *Davis*
linia, 1480, part of Sir John Mandivilles travels,
cuts, b l. printed by Wynkyn de Worde, 1563

1355 compendium biblie quod aureum alias biblie repor- _ 3. 6 *D.Hunter*
torum nuncupatur, m. b.

1356 tractatus Auguftini in libro de fpiritu et littera, &c. 1. _ . _ *Thane*
g. l. nitid.

1357 ——— de fpheræ, angeli concordantie aftronomie, _ 12. _ *D.Hunter*
fig, m. b 1490

1358 regimen fanitatis Salerni, m b. tractatus de facra- _ 9. _
mentis, m b 1492

1359 opere di Dolce, tratte de Ovidio, con. fig. Ven. 1568 - 1. 6

1360 hiftoria Jo. Majorem de geftis et Scotorum, m. g. l. _ 5. 6 *D.º*
ex officiana afcenfiana 1521

1361 opufculum Auguftini, quod vulgo Dacus Major, m. — 4. _ *Macarty*
b. and 1 more

1362 An. Cælafpini demonum inveftigatio, Florent, ap. - 16. _ *D.Hunter*
Juntas, 1530, and 5 more

L. v. d
59. 7. 6

Capt. Bretwell — 8. 6 1363 Nauseæ libri mirabilium septem, cum fig. m. b Col. ap. Quentell, 1532, prognosticatio Jo. Liechtenbergers, cum fig. m. b. Colon. ap Quentell, 1526

Bud. — *2.6 ** 1363 Tonstalli in laudem matrimonio, m. g. b. ap. Freben. Basil, 1519, Huldricus Zuinglius ad Marrinum Lutherum, m. g. l. 1527

—. *2.6* 1364 vitæ 230 summorum pontificum, m. b. 1507, Buchius de elementis literariis, &c. m. b. Colon. per Quentell, 1520

Cater —. *5.—*1365 Maturentii de componendis carminibus opusculum, &c. m. g l. Venet.1493, Chappusii de mente & memoria, &c ap Assen. 1515

—. *2.6* 1366 Valentini de institutione fœminæ christianæ m. g. l. Colon. 1524, Matheii Fontinis opuscula varia, m. g. l. 1502

—. *2.6* 1367 institutio principis christiani, Erasmo, m. g. l. Basil, 1516, de regis officio, opusculum, m. b. Paris, ap. H. Steph. 1519

Nicol —. *6.6* 1368 passionarius Galeni, m. g. l. 1526, Lelandi assertio Arturii regis Britannie, m. b. Lond 1544

—. *2. —* 1369 Cassiodori Senat. de regem. ecclef primitive hysoria, nitid. g. l. Bonaventure tractatus de tribus ternariis peccat infamibus, &c. g. l.

Cater, —. *8.—*1370 Guevara's familiar and golden epistles, b. l. by Fenton, m. g. l. impr. by Newberie, 1577

Thane *1.10.—*1371 the cronicles of Englonde, b. l. (the first edit.) imperfect, printed by Caxton, 1480

Mason *2.9.—*1372 orationes devotissimæ Christo dicatæ virginique deiparæ, a curious MS on vellum, with 32 cuts, finely illuminated *Copper plates colored*

Shrobshire *9.—-*1373 a very curious MS on vellum of husbandry, gardening, and old English poetry, supposed to be wrote by Humphrey the good duke of Glaucester, with a fine portrait of his duchess, on the side. N. B. See Mr. West's MS of this book before the title

Capt. Bretwell *3. 3.* 1374 a genealogical manuscipt roll on vellum from Adam to Henry the VIth finely illuminated, supposed to have been extracted by the monks as a compliment to that king, 9 yards long, in a tin case, an unit, and very curious

Shroffhire *9.—-*1375 a pedigree of the families of the Sparowes and Martin iu Essex and Suffolk, in the 22d year of Henry the VIth, a MS roll on vellum, illuminated

Capt. Bretwell *10.—.—*1376 an Incian manuscipt on paper, shewing how they keep their histories, &c in boards

F O L I O.

£. s. d

96 -9.

1377 Tindal, Frith, and Barnes's works imper. b, l, by _ .*10.* _ *Marly*
Daye, 1572, and 2 biles, b, l.

1378 Biblia Sacra, 1543, Gefneri bibliotheca univerfalis _ .*10 .6* *Nicol*

1379 rerum Anglicarum fcriptores poft Bedam, Lond. _. *11.6* *Dampii*
1595, Lombardica hyftoria, 1485, and 2 more

1380 Gregorii Byzantinæ hiftoriæ, Gr. et Lat. Bafil, _ *2.6* *Nicol.*
1562, Alfoidi annales ecclefiæ Anglicanæ, Lcod.
1663

1381 Eromenia, or love and revenge, by Hayward, 1632, - *2.* _*Chapman*
and 3 more

1382 Suetoni hiftoria Beroaldi, Salluftii opera, 1514, and. .*2.* _ *Nicol*
1 more

1383 deftruƈtorium viciorum, Paris, 15 9, magcumetis, - .*2.* _ *Chapman*
vitæ ac alcoram, cum confutationes, 1550, and 2
more

1384 Bp Burnet's hiftory of his own time vol. 1ft l. p. _ *13.* _*Cater*
1724, hiftoire Militaire de Eugene and Malborough
v. 3d fewed

1385 Manton's fermons, &c. 4 v. _ _ _ _ _ - -.*15.* *Burnell*

1386 the Holy Bible, b. l, 2 v. m, b, g, l, imperfeƈt 1549} /. *11.6*

1387 another copy, by Coverdale, cuts imper. g, l,

1388 biblia facra, m, g, l, Venetiis, per Leonardum Wild - .*18.* _ *Woods*
1481

1389 the great book of ftatutes to the 34 year of Henry - .*11.* _ *Nicol*
VIII, b, l, m, b,

1390 old ftatutes to the time of Edward the IVth m. g.l. _. *11.* _
prin. by Machlinia *Without name & Date*

1391 Hall's chronicle, b, l, m g, l, Printed by Grafton /. -. _*Cater*
1548

1392 the paftyme of people, the chronicles of dyvers *4. 7*
realmys, b. l. feveral leaves wrote, with wood cuts *Dr Chauncey*
m, g, l, by J. Raftell *No 1013*

1393 the cronicles of Englonde, b, l, m. g, l, a fine copy *5.5.* _*F.*
prin. by Caxton

1394 cronycle of Englonde, with the fruyt of tymes, b, l, *7. 7.* *Dr Hunter*
m, printed at Saynte Albones 1483

1395 ftatuta ap, weftmonaft edito anno primo repis Ricard *3. 3.* _ *Thane*
Tercii m. g, l, by Caxton no date

1396 Turner's herball, b. l. a fine copy, 1568 _. *18.* _

1397 the grete herball, b, l, c. r. imp. by John Kynge, - .*10.6* *Collison*

1398 Bullen's bulwarke of defence againft all ficknes, b. - .*5.6* *Durham.*
m, b, imp, by Kyngfton, 1562

1399 the vertuoufe booke of diftyllacyon, b. l. by Jerom - .*12.* _
Brunfwicke, with wood cuts, c. r. imp. by Law-
rens Andrewe 1577

£. s. d

126. 17. –

D: Hornlor –	10 – 1400	the judycyall of uryns, b. l. no date, m. g l.
–. 13.6	1401	Geminum's anatomie, with 39 cuts, b. l m b, Grey. impr. 1559
2.18 –	1402	the kalendayr of the fhyppars, b. l. with wood cuts WL. 1503
2.10. –	1403	Barclay's fhyp of folys, b. l. cuts, m. g. l. a, fine D: Chauncy copy, by Pynfon, 1508
1. –. –	1404	liber feftivalis, b. l. m, g. l imp. by Pynfon.
1-.6. –	1405	Dives and Pauper, that ss to fay the riche and the F. pore, b. l. m g, l imp. by Pynfon, 1493
–. 11.6	1406	leteltum tenuris new corecte, b. l. m. g. l. imp. by Thane Pynfon, 1516
–. 7.6	1407	ftatuta anno 11th of king Henry VII, m. b. printed D.º by Wynkyn de Worde
1.1. –	1408	the elements of Euclide, by Dee, c. t. Lond. printed D: Hunter by Daye, 15·0, with the portrait of the printer
–. 10.6	1409	Digges's pantometria, m. g. l. printed by Jeffes 1591 Nicol
–. 13. –	1410	Batman uppon Bartholome, his booke de proprieta- Cater tibus rerum, b. l. m. g. l. a fine copy, London imp. by Thomas Eaft 1582
–. 8. –	1411	the interchangeable courfe, er variety of things in Nicol. the whole world, very fcarce, printed by Charles Yetfweirt, Efq; 1594
–. 10. –	1412	Hackluyt's voyages, b, l. imperf. m. b, imprinted by Barker 1589
–. 11. –	1413	the hiftorie of Scanderbeg, king of Albanie, m. g l. BWhite 1596
– 19. –	1414	the boke callyd the myrroure of oure ladv, very ne- Nicol ceffarye for all religyous perfones, b. l a fine copy, in the original binding, imp. by Fakes 1530
1.4. –	1415	the works of Geffray Chaucer, b. l printed by Toye, Brando 1546
–. 9.6	1416	the myrrour or glafs of Chriftes paffion, b, l. imp. WL. by Redman, 1534, the boke of common prayer, b, l. imp by Grafton 1549
–. 7.6	1417	les annales d'Aquitaine, faictz & geftes de roys de Dalby France & d'Angleterre et des pays de Naples & de Milan, Paris, par Jaques Bouchet, imprimeur
2.2. –	1418	Omeliæ Gregoriæ papæ, g, l. Paris 1475 Thane
–. 7. –	1419	homiliæ, impreffæ Spiræ 1482 Dº
– 18. –	1420	miffale ad ufum infignis ecclefie Sarifburienfis, cum VH. fig. 6 t. g, l. Paris ap Merlin 1555
–. 9. –	1421	Cantemir's hiftory of the Othman empire, by Tin- dal, cuts, m, b. g, l. 1734
2.2. –	1422	the copye of a letter whyche maiftre Alavn Charre- Nicol tier wrote to hys brother, whyche defired to dwell

L. s. d
149 -. -

in court, with the many miferyes and wretchyd-
neffes therein, by Wylliam Caxton, very fair

1422 here begyaneth the lyf of the holy and bleifid vyrgyn *Only 15 lines* 2.17. - *Nicol*
faynt Wenefrede, printed by Caxton

1423 the boke of Eneydos compylcd by Vyrgyle, b l. m. 5.5. - *D.º*
g, l. by Caxton 1490

1424 Troylus and Crefeyde, imperf. b. l. m g. l. by Cax- 2. -. - *WH*
ton

1424 fpeculum vite Crifti, perfect, m, g, l, emprynted by 3.10. - *Thane*
Caxton

1426 the doctrinal of fapyence, the whyche is ryght, utile 8.8. *Shropfhire*
and prouffyttable to alle Cryften men, b, l. m, g, l.
by Caxton 1489

1427 the boke called Cathon, b. l. m, g, l. by ditto 1483 5.5. *D. Hunter*

1428 The polytyque boke, named Tullius de fenectute, in 14. -. - *Nicol.*
Englyfhe, *b. l.* by Caxton, Tullius de Amicicia, in
Englisfh, m. g. l. ditto 1481

1429 the game of cheffe playe, *b. l.* m. g. l. ditto 1474 16. -. - *D.º*

1430 the boke that is callyd fefcival the yere of our Lorde, 3.2. -
1486, fome leaves wrote very neat, printed by
Caxton

1431 the moft vertuoufe hyftorye of the devoute and righi 3.15. - *Nicol.*
renown d lyves of holy faders lyyying in deferte,
b, l, with wood cuts, by Caxton *W. de Worde* 1495

1432 Queene Elizabeth's pfalms with the tunes, b, l, m, b, -.12. -
impr. by Day 1565

1433 a manufcript on vellum, in verfe -.10. -

1434 Chambers's dictionary, 2 vols. neat 1741 3.3. -

1435 legenda fanctorum, in Englifh, a manufcript, on vel- 4.9. -
lum, fairly wrote, and the capitals illuminated

End of the Eighth Day's Sale,   £ 238 10 -

K

Ninth Day's Sale,

SATURDAY, APRIL 6, 1776.

L. s. d

Floyer — . 1. — 1436 INTRODUCTION a la vie devote, par de Sales, and 8 more

Brander — . 3. — 1437 Alciati emblemata, cum fig. and 6 more

WH. — . 10. — 1438 Moulton's myrror, or glaffe of health, b. l. and 17 more, impr. by Eliz. Redman

Brander — . 8. — 1439 the pyftles and gofpels, b. l. cuts, Paris, 1538, and 10 more

D°. — . 5. — 1440 Wither's fatyrical effays, abufes ftript and whipt, 1622, and 14 more

B. White — . 6. — 1441 a catalogue of the curious library of the late James Weft, Efq; interleaved, and 4 more

D°. — . 10. 6 1442 tooth-leffe fatyres, m. g. l. 1598, the fcourge villanie, newe fatyres, c. t. g. l. 1599, and 1 more

— . 3. — 1443 Blundeville of counfells and councellors, m. b. and 2 more

Mecham — . 16. — 1444 the voyce of the laft trumpet, b. l. m. b. impr. by Crawley, 1550, and 4 more

— . 4. — 1445 Goffon's fchoole of abufe, b. l. m. b. Lond. impr. by Woodcocke, 1587, Seager's fchoole of vertue, b. l. m. b. by Seares, 1557, and 2 more

WH — . 4. 6 1446 the world poffeffed with black and white devils, b. l. impr. by Perin, 1583, and 4 more

Brander — . 8. — 1447 a fruiteful and pleafant worke of Sir T. More, called utopia, b. l. m. g. l. impr. by Vele, 1551, the goodly hiftory of the beautyful lady Lucres of Scene, b. l. impr. by Kynge, 1560, the ende of the Jane Dudley, b. l. m. g. l. and 1 more

D°. 4. 6 1448 the trewe differens between the regal and the ecclef. power, by Stafforde, b. l. m. g. l. impr. by Copland, 1548, Joye of the end of the worlde, b. l. m. g. l. 1548

(75)

£. s. d.

3 . 17. 6

1449 an exhortation to the Scotts to conforme them- -- .13. _ *Nicol*
felves to the union between the two realms, *b. l.*
neat, printed by Gratton, 1547, and 1 more

1450 the ofspring of the houfe of Ottomanno, pertaining -- .6. _ *D°*
to the greate Turkes court, *b. l. m. g. l.* impr. by
Marihe, 1553. the kynge of England's title to
Scotland, *b. l. m. g l.*   1548

1451 introduction to wifdome, baket of fapience, *b. l.* - .1. 6
and 2 more

1452 the Newe Teftament yet once agayne corrected, *b.* _ .6.6 *WH.*
l. cuts, printed in the low countries, in 1528 or
29 Tyndal begun this tranflation in 1525

1453 the Newe Teftament with notes, *m g. l.* printed by - .13. _
Badius, at Geneva,   1557.

1454 the primer of king Henry the VIIIth, *b. l.* perfect _. 8. _ *WH.*
and very fcarce, impr. by Mayler,   1539

1455 the book of common prayer, *m b* very fcarce, - 7
impr by Barker, 1596, the Newe Teftament, with
Beza's notes, *m. g. l.* impr. by Barker, 1586, and
1 more

1456 the nomenclator or remembrancer of Adrianus Ju--- .3. 6 *Cozens*
nius, in Latine, Greeke, Frenche; Englifh d by
Higins, m. g. l. impr. by Newberie,   1585

1457 pithy pleafant and profitable works of maiftre - .9. _ *Dalby*
Skelton; *b. l.* 1568, the court of virtue, *b. l.* 1565

1458 the metamorphofis of Pigmalions image and cer- -- .5. _
tuine fatyres, 1598, and 2 more

1459 the gerlande of godly flowers, b. l. m. g. l. impr. - 4.6 *Howe*
by Will. Howe, 1574, St. Auguftine of the love
of God, b. l. neat,   1570

1460 Select prayers out of St. Auguftine's meditations,- .11. _ *Mole*
b. l. m g. l. printed by Daye,   1574

1461 Beza's pithy fumme of the chriftian fayth, b. l. m. -- .5. _ *Brander*
g. l. impr. by Waldegrave, 1585, Mornay's trea-
tife of the church, b. l. m, g. l. impr. by Barker,
1581

1462 the image of governaunce, Englys'd by Elyote, *b l.* - .6. _ *D°*
neat, 1556, Xenophon's treatife of houfeholde, b.
l. m. b. impr. by Berthelet,   1537

1463 Sebaftian Munfter's ftraunge and memo able things, - .14. _ *Grey*
b. l m. g l. impr by Marfhe, 1574, Ribaut's laft
voyage to Terra Florida, *b. l.* neat, impr. by
Denham

1464 Julius Cæfar's commentaries, *b. l.* impr. by Ceres, _ .6. *Meeham.*
1565, and 1 more

£. s. d.
8. 19. –

Mole —. 2.6 1465 an abridgement of the notable woorke of Polidore
11 Virgile, by Langley, b. l. m. g. l. impr. by Grafton, 1546

Brander — 7.6 1466 another copy, b. l. m. g. l. impr. by Tisdale, an
16 extracte of examples, apothemes, and histories,
collected out of Brusonius, &c. b. l. m. g. l. impr.
by Bynneman, 1572

Nicol — 4 –1467 Tullius Ciceroes bookes of duties, by Grimalde, b.
— 4 – l. impr. by Tottell, 1558, the golden Booke of
Marcus Aurelius, b. l. neat, impr. by East, 1586

Do — 6 – 1468 the breviarv of Eutropius, Englished by C. W. b. l.
— 5 6 m. b. impr. by Bynneman, 1568

Do .2.6 1469 Marke Tullye Ciceroe's fyve tusicular questions,
— .6.– Englished by Dolman, b. l. impr by Marshe,
1561, booke of frendshippe, &c. b l neat, 1577

Do —. 5. 1470 the first tragedie of L. A. Seneca, bv Heywood,
b l. m. g· l. impr. by Sutton, 156 , sixth tragedie
of Seneca, by ditto, b. l. m g. l. impr, by Tot-
till, 1559

—· 4. –1471 the flowers of Terence, selected by Udall, b l. m.
g l. impr. by Marshe, 1581, Ovide's pistel's, by
Turberville, b. l m. b. impr. by Denham.

—. 5. 6 1472 heir beginnis the sevin seages translatit out of Prois
in Scottis meiter by Jhon Rolland in Dalkeith,
b. l. Edinb. printit by Robert Smyth, 1592

QUARTO.

—. 8.6 1473 the life and death of Martin Luther, with his portrait, 1641, and 3 more v. of scarce tracts.

Brander —. 6.6 1474 a collection of historical tracts, in the time of
Charles the Ist, and Oliver Cromwell 9 v.

—. 5.6 1475 Raleigh's prerogative of parliaments in England,
1640 and 7 more

Collins —. 12 – 1476 the owles almanack, 1618, a herryngs tayle, 1598,
and 10 more very curious

Chapman —. 4. –1477 Carew's survey of Cornwall, 1602, Smyth de republica Anglorum, 1583, and 3 more

WWhite —. 4.6 1478 the diail of Daies, by Lloid, b. l, 1590, and 4 more

Collins —. 13 .–1479 Higgins's myrreur for magistrates, b. l, imperf and
9 curious pamphlets

Mole —. 5.6 1480 the armorie of honour, cuts, b. l, colour'd, imperf. and
2 more

—. 2.6 1481 Levins's dictionarie of English and Latine words, b.
l, 1570, and 2 more

Brander —. 2. –1482 Wilson's arte of rhetorique and logique, b. l, 1533

15. -. -

1483 determination on King Henry the 8th's marriage, b. - . 15. - . Brander
l, imp. by Berthelet, 1531, the boke named the go-
vernour, by Sir Thomas Elyot, b. l, imp. by Berthelet, 1531

1484 the art of riding, fet foorth, by Xenophon and Gry- - 5. 6 Nicol
fon, g. l, imp. by Denham   1584

1485 Blondeville's fower chiefyft offices belonging to - 9. - Dᵃ
horfemanfhippe, b. l, m, g. l, cuts. imp by Seres

1486 the pathwaie to martiall difcipline, by Styward, b. l, - 17. - Dᵉ
m, g. l, 1582, inftructions, obfervations and orders
mylitarie, by Smyth, b. l, m. b.   1595

1487 Digges's militare treatife, named ftratifoticos, b. l, - 16. -
m. b. printed by Bynneman, 1579, the practice of
fortification, by Ive, cuts, b. l, m, g. l.   1585

1488 a martial conference betweene Captain Skil and Cap- - 11. -
tain Pill, by Barnabe Rich, b. l, m. b, 1598, and
2 more

1489 inftructions for the warres, by monf. de Bellay, tranf- - 11. - Dᵉ
lated by Ive, b. l, m, g. l, 1,89, an allarme to Eng-
land, by Rich, b. l, m, g. l.   1578

1490 a profitable booke concerning navigation, by Eden, - 8. -
b. l, m. b, imp. by Jugge, a pleafaunt recreation for
navigators, compyled by Blagrave, b. l, m, b,
1598

1491 the ufe of the familiar ftaffe, b l, m. b, by Blagrave, 2. 6
1590, the art of dialling, by Fale, b. l, m. b, printed
by Orwin ———— 1593

1492 Digges's pantometria, longimetra & ftercometria, b. - . 8 - Dʳ Hunter
l, m, g. l, imp. by Bynneman, 1571, a profitable
arte of dyeing fylkes, &c. b. l.   1588

1493 Mountaine's gardener's labyrinth, cuts, b. l, m, g. l, 1. 2. - Barker
imp. by Bynneman, 1577, Hill's profitable arte of
gardening, b. l, m. b, by Bynneman   1574

1494 the profitable fcience of furveying landes, by Leigh, - 9. 6 Dᶜ
b. l, m. b, 1577, the brooke of hufbandry, by Fitzherbert, b. l, m. b, and one more

1495 the golden boke of Marcus Aurelius, b. l, finely - 14. - Dʳ Hunter
bound ———— 1535

1496 Latymer's frutefull fermons, b. l, m, g. l, printed by - 8. 6 Brander
Daye ———— 1578

1497 Bede's hiftory of the church of Englande, by Staple- - 6. - Dᵇ
ton, b. l, m, g. l.   1565

1498 another copy, b. l, m, g. l.   1565 - 5. 6 Hayes

1499 Cooper's chronicle, b. l, m, g. l.   1569 - 18. 6 Mok

£. s. d
24. 4. –

D *Hunter*	– *19.* –	**1500** Carion's chronicles, b. l, m, g. l.	1550
	– *. 6.* –	1501 Afcham's toxophilus, the fchoole of fhooting, b. l, m, g. l, ——	1589
	– *. 7.* –	1502 ——'s fchole mafter, b. l, m, g. l, imp. by Daye,	1571
Cozens	– *7. 6*	1503 Guevara's diall of princes, by North, b. l, m, g. l, imp by Tottill ——	1582
Nicol	*5* –	1504 the droome of Doomes day, by Gafcoigne, b. l, m. b.	1556
D°	– *17.* –	1505 Cortes's pleafant hiftorie of the conqueft of Weft-India, by North, b, l, m, g, l, printed by Creede,	1596
D. Hunter	– *. 14.* –	1506 the hiftorie of travayle in the Weft and Eaft-Indies, by Eden, b. l, m, g, l, imp, by Jugge	1577
Dalby	– *. 8.* –	1507 the navigations, peregrinations and voyages of Nicholay, tranfl ted by Wafhington, cuts, b, l, m, imp, by Dawfon	1585
Brander	– *.11.* –	1508 the inftitution of a chriften man, or interpretation of the crede, &c. b, l, m, g. l, imp, by Berthelet,	1537
	– *. 6. 6*	1509 Bale's pageant of popes, b, l, m, b, imp, by Marfhe,	1574
D. Morrell	– *. 7.* –	1510 Florio's garden of recreation, Italian proverbes, &c. m, g l, ——	1591
Mann	– *. 3. 6*	1511 Fletcher's profitable fimile, b l, a treatife of mathematical phificke by judiciall aftronomy, printed by Purtoot ——	1598
Nicol	– *. 4.* –	1512 a locking glaffe for the unlearned, by Flemming, b l, imp by Newberie, 1576, the mirrour of policie, for magiftrates, &c.	1598
D°	– *14.* –	1513 a regiftre of hyftories, written by Elianus, tranflated bp Fleming, b l, m, g l, imp. by Woodcocke,	1576
Cozens	– *. 2. 6*	1514 the hyftorie of Juftine, tranflated by Golding, b l, m b, imp. by Marfhe	1578
Nicol	– *. 8.* –	1515 Julius's Cæfar's commentaries, tranflated by Golding, b l, m, g l, imp. by Efte	1590
D°	– *.12.* –	1516 the orationes of Demofthenes, Englyfh'd by Wilfon, b l, m, g l, impr by Denham	1570
D°	– *.12.* –	1517 the hiftory of Herodian, tranflated by Smyth, b l, m, g l, impr by Copland	
Grey	/ *5.* –	1518 the confpiracie of Catiline, tranflated by Paynell, b l, m, g l, by Berthelet	1541

£. s. d.
33 .13. —

1519 the hiftorie of Quintus Curtius, tranflated by Brende, — .17. —DʳHunter
b l, m, g l impr by Tottell   1561

1520 the auncient order, focietie and unitie laudable of /. ⁴. — Knight
Prince Arthure and his knightly armory of the
of the round table, by Robinfon, b l, impr by Wolfe,
1583

1521 Aurelia, the paragon of pleafuru and princeiy de- —.14 —Mayers
lights, b l, m, g l,   1593

1522 the hiftorie of Italye, by Thomas, b l, m, g l, impr — . 10. —Brander
by Marfhe   1561

1523 another copy, b l, m, g l, Berthelet   1549 — ./5. —

1524 the praife of folie, by Erafmûs, b l, m, g l, impr by — ./3. — Nicol
Berthelet   1549

1525 the difcoverie and conqueft of Peru, cuts, by Nicho- — .19. —Knight
las, b, l.   1581

1526 a difcovery of the fubtill practife of the Spanifh in- — .4. 6 Mecham
quifition, b. l. m. b. J. Day   1568

1527 Shute's notable commentaries of the Turkes and em- — .8. — Cater.
pire, b, l, m, g, l, Hall   1562

1528 a fruteful and pleafant book called the inftruction of — .9. —Knight
a chriften woman, by Hýrde, b, l, m, g, l, Wykes.
1557

1529 Reignold's lives of the Roman emperors, b, l, Marfhe, — .4. 6 White
1571

1530 the droome of doomes day, by Gafcoigne, b l, c r, — . 6.——
1576

1531 the nyne fyrft bookes of the Eneidos of Virgil, by — .8. —DʳHunter
Phaer, b l, m g l   1562

1532 the civile converfation of Guazzo, by Pettie, b l, — .?. —Brander
m g l, Eaft   1586

1533 delectable demaundes and pleafant queftions in mat- — .16. Knight
ters of love, b l, m, g l, Creede   1596

1534 the golden boke of Marcus Aurelius, b l, very fair, — .10. — Nicol
Berthelet   1538

1535 Guevara's familiar epiftles and chronicle, b l, New- — .8. — Cater
berie   1577

1536 a righte noble and pleafant hiftory of Alexander the — .11. — Mole
Great, by Stocker, b l, Bynneman   1569

1537 beautiful bloffomes gathered by John Bifhop from — .6. — Tutt
the beft of trees of all kyndes,   b l m b, 1577

1538 the boke of Boetius called the comfort of philofo- /. /. —Knight
phye, by Colvile, b l, m, g l, Cawoode   1566

1539 the bookes of the golden afs of Apuleius, by Adling- — ./1. — Nicol.
ton, b l, m b, Howe   1571

45 . 9 . 6

-. **.** - 1540 a boke of godly praiers, with cuts, b l, m b   *Tutet*

- . *II.* - 1541 the boke of the inſtruction of a chriſten women, *Bartlet*
b l, m b, Berthelet, 1541, an harborowe againſt
a late blowne blaſte concerning the governement of
wemen, Straſhorow

- *5.* - 1542 Tyndale's parable of the wicked mammon, b l, *Cater*
Hans Luft   1528

-. *4.6* 1543 Biſhop Fiſher uppon the ſeaven penytentyal pſalmes, *Tutet*
b l, m b, Pynſon   1510

- *3* - 1544 Bp Hooper's anſwer to Bp Gardiner's book intytled
a deteccion of the devyls ſophiſtrye, b l, neat 1547

-. *10.* - 1545 the image of governance of Alexander Severus, by *Chapman*
Eliot, b l, Berthelet, 1541, the moral philoſophie
of Doni by North, cuts, b l, m b, Denham 1570

-. *12.* - 1546 the travailes and adventures of Don Simonides, by *Nicol*
B. Riche, b l, m b, Walley, 1584, Gilberte's diſ-
coverie for a new paſſage to Cataia, b l, m b Middleton   1576

-. *9. 6* 1547 Newnam's night crowe, a bird that breedeth braules *Bartlet*
in many families and houſholdes, b. l. m, b, by
Wolfe, 1590, Holland's treatiſe againſt witchcraft
m, b. Legatt,   Camb 1590

-. *6.6* 1548 a diſcourſive probleme concerning prophecies, by *WH.*
Harvey, b, l, m, b, 1588, a treatiſe of juſtification
founde emonge the writinges of Card. Pole, m, b,
Lovanii, 1569

-. *5. 6* 1549 Paſquine in a traunce, containing ſtraung newes out *Mecham*
of Heaven, purgatorie and Hell, b. l. m. b. imp.
by Eaſt,   1584

-. *6.6* 1550 anorher copy, m, b, Seres - - - - - - *Hayes*

-. *8.* - 1551 Phlotimus the warre betwixt nature and fortune, by *Brandir*
milbancke, b, l, m, b, 1583, Eunapius, of the
lives of philoſophers, and oratours, b, l,   1579

- *7.* - 1552 the courtyer of caſtilio, Englyſh'd by Hoby, b, l, *Nicol*
m, b, 1561, the quinteſence of wit by Hichcock,
b, l, m, b, Aldde,   1590

/. /. . - 1553 the flower of fame, containing the fortunate reigne
of Henry the VIIIth, in verſe by Fulwell, b, l, m,
b, Hoſkins, 1575, and 2 more

- -. *4.* - 1554 the eſtate of Engliſh fugitives under the King of *Tutet*
Spaine, &c. m, b, 1596, a narration of the de-
ſtruction of the Indes by the Spanyards, b, l, m, b,
1583

£. s. d.
51. P. 6

1555 Lopez's report of the Kingdome of Congo, a region _ .6. _ Chapman
of Africa, by Hartwell, the conqueſt of the Eaſt-
Indias, tranſlated by Frampton, b, l, m, b, 1579

1556 the aſſize of bread, cuts, b, l, m, b, Windet, 1597 - .10. _ Bartlett
and 1 more

1557 of the knowledge and conducte of warres, m, b, _.7. 6 Cozens
Tottell, 1578, the manſion of Magnanimitie, by
Crompton, b, l, m, b, Ponſonby, 1599 and 1 more

1558 Heywood's epigrammes, b, l, 1587, the ſeven firſt - .12. _ Mann
bookes of the eneidos of virgill, by Phaer, b, l,
1558, the mirour for magiſtrates, b, l, 1574

1559 a collection of ſtatutes from Magna Carta to 1557, _ .1. 6 Tutet
b. l. by Tottell, and 1 more 1559

1560 the booke of diſtillations, by Barker, cuts, b, l, neat _ .3. _ Chapman
Short, 1599

1561 the conſent of time, diſciphering the errors of the _ .14. _ Nicol
Grecians in their olympiads, by Lloid, b, l, m, g,
l, impr. by Biſhon 1590

1562 the three partes of commentaries, of the civill warres - .6. 6 Cater
of Fraunce, tranſlated by Timme, b, l, Coldocke,
1574

1563 painter's palace of pleaſure, hiſt. tragical matters - .8. -
&c. b, l, vol. 2d, 1567, Fenton's tragical diſ-
courſes, b, l, wants the title 1567

1564 Buckingham's works, v. 2d, 1723, Pope's eſſay on _ .7. 6 Cozens
man 1724

1565 Stukeley's medallic hiſtory of Carauſius, book 2d, _ .5. 6 Cater
1759, and 1 more

1566 regni Angliæ reginæ Elizabethæ religio & Guber- _ .3. _ W
uatio eccles. typis T. Wood, Lond. 1729, and 2
more

1567 Pierce's law and equity of the goſpel, c t, g l, 1680 _ .3. _ Cater

1568 ephemeris expeditionis Norreſſii & Drakii in luſita- _ .7. 6 Collins
niam, m b, 1589, Queſtiones Johannis Dedicus,
artuum liberalium triump, philoſophiarum, &c.
Oxon. John Scolar, and 3 more

1569 Whittintoni de octo partibus oratonis, b l, Winan- _ 7. _ Howell
dum de Worde, 1691, Lambardi de Priſcis Anglo-
rum Legibus, b l, m b, Day, 1568, and 3 more

1570 Herbarius maguntie impreſſus, cum fig. Colorat. _ .12. _ Dr. Hunter
1571 Eraſmi Enarratio in primun Pſalmum davidicum, _ .5. 6 Macarty,
1515, Lillii Grægorii Ziral di Ferranenſis ſyntagma
de muſis, 1512, Abr. Judaei Tractatus de nativita-
tibus, 1545 and 2 more

L

L.s.d
57.8.—

(82)

Mann — . *1.6* 1572 Hen. Cor. Agrippa de occulta philofophia lib, tres,
antv. 1531, P. Vergilii de Rerum Inventioribus,
Paris ap. Rob. Stephi 1528
Chapman — . *3.6* 1573 Bayfius de re Navali, Paris ap. Rob. Steph, 1536
and 2 more
Dr Harwood — . *13.* 1574 Æliani de militaribus ordinibus inftituendis, cum
fig. Græce, Venet 1552, variæ hiftoriæ, &c. Græce
Romæ, 1545 and 1 more
WI. — . *3.6* 1575 Liber feftivalis opus regale, Ludg, 1508
Brander — . *1.6* 1576 dictionarium chaldaicum, Bafil. ap. Froben 1527
Dr Hunter — . *1.* — 1577 Avicenna opera medici 1522
Fox. — . *2.* — 1578 Eufebii praparatione Evangelica 1480
Dampier — . *5.6* 1579 fpaeti ravennetis & de origine amplitudine de vaſtatione & de inftauvratione urbis Ravennæ, Venet.
1489
Gough — . *4.* — 1580 directorum facerdſtum, fatifburienfis, per me Richardum Pynfon, 1528
D°. — . *11.* — 1581 horæ beatiffime virginis Marie eccles, Sarifbureinſis
per Pynfon, 1522
— *3.* — 1582 hiftoriarum camaldu lenfuim lib. tres, Aug. Florentino Monacho Camaldulenfe Auctore, m, g. l,
Florent, 1575
Dampier — *7.6* 1583 natura brevium b l, and 11 more
Tulet — . *4.* — 1584 an old b l, Bible and 1 more
Brander — . *5.* — 1585 la Couftume de Normandie, Roven, 1512, and 4
more
Bartlett — . *6.6* 1586 Doboen's herball, b l, 1595, touchftone of complexions, 1633, a difference betwene an Englifh and
Hebrew witch 1653
Brander — . *16.* — 1587 Boetii confolatione philofophiæ, a manufcript on
paper
D°. — . *10.* — 1588 legenda aurea, a mfs on vellum
D°. — . *7.* — 1589 a miffale, a mfs on vellum illuminated
Howard. *2.4.* — 1590 hiftoria general. Anglorum ecclefiaft. a mfs on vellum
Brander *1.* — . — 1591 liber pfalmorum, &c. a MS on vellum illuminated
Dr Hunter *6.16.6* 1592 Bede expofitio in epiftolas apoftoli, a MS on vellum,
2 v m. g l.
WI. — . *2.6* 1593 fpeculum fpiritualium, & opufculum Richardi Hampole, m b. 1512
Cozens — . *2.* — 1594 inftitutiones imperiales, g l. Paris, per Udalricum,
1499
Dr Hunter. *1.* — . — 1595 le grant voyage de Jherufalem, m. g l. Paris, per
Regnault, 1517

MANUSCRIPTS.

£. s. d
73. 19. _

1596 A stately poem, called, the destruction of Troy, *4. 1. 6 Dʳ Hunte* wrote by Joseph of Exeter, who lived in the reign of king Henry IId, 1154, to 1189, and 3 more

1597 the lady Alice Oldfield her Kallicia & Philædus, and *1 2. 6 Brander* 6 more

1598 five on vellum, folio, &c. _ _ _ _ _ *4. 5. _ Dᵒ*

FODIO.

1599 five Stukely on the spleen, in quires, cuts, 1723 _ *11. _ Mgle*

1600 a collection of old statutes, b. l. 6 v. printed by _ *5. _ Tutet* Wykes, Jugge, Cawood Pynson, &c, 1502, 1559, &c.

1691 Grafton's chronicle, imperfect, 1568, chronique de _ *14. _ Cater* Froissart, tom. 1ſt imp.

1692 Fox's book of martyrs, b l. Daye, 1576, with the _ *10. _* portrait of the printer, Purchas his pilgrimes, v. 2d.
                                    1625
1603 Grafton's chronicle, b l. imperfect, 1563, and 4 more *1. _. _,*

1604 Erasmu's paraphrase on the New Testament, 2 v. _ *7. _ Tutet* b l. 1548, and 1 more

1605 Guevara's dial of princes, by North, b l. Tottell, _ *7. 6 Dᵒ* 1558, Vigon's woorkes of chirurgery, b l. 1550

1606 speculum historiale vincentii, Venet. 1494, Linde- _ *19. _ Fox* wode, provinciales editio antiqua, 1433, and 1 more

1607 rerum in ecclef. gestarum, a Foxo Basil, per oporium, _ *4. _* and 3 more

1608 origines ſſi antiquitates Germaniſis, per Herold, Ba- _ *5. _ Cater* fil, 1557, Polybyii historia, &c. in edibus Afcen- fianis, 1512, and 3 more

1609 Erasmi annotationes in Nov. Testamentum, Bafil, _ *6. 6 Chapman* 1519, bibliotheca Eliotæ, Lat. & Eng. impr. 1548, and 2 more

1610 Speculum de confeffione, Lovaniæ, 1488, livres des *3. 6 Macarty* illuftrations de Gaule, and 2 more

1611 Con. Lycofthenem de prodigiis & oftentis, cum fig. *2. 10. Dʳ Monro* and 5 more

1612 Baarlandi Hollandiæ comitum hiftoriæ & icones, *1. 3. Crukſhanks* 1584, and 3 more

1613 Sir Thos. More's felect pieces, b l. 1557, and 2 _ *16. Knight* more

_ℓ.s.d_
_90. 13.6_

£.s.d
107.2. —

1639 flores hiftoriarum Matthæi Weftmonaft. 1567 — *6.6*
1640 Bede hiftoria ecclefiaftica, gent. Aglorum, m b, 1500,— *3. Connaught*
  idem liber nitid Antw. 1550
1641 Rofa Anglica practica medicine Venet 1416 — *15. Bartlat*
1642 Biblia facra 1500 — *10.6 Lee*
1643 Cranmer's anfwer to Gardiner, *b. l.* impr. by Wolfe, — *5.6 Brander*
  1551
1644 Another copy, *m. g. l.* impr. by Daye, 1580 — *9. Nible*
1645 Marlorate on St. Matthew, by Tymme, *b. m. b.* — *4.6 Bartlat*
  impr. by Marfhe, 1570
1646 Gualthere's homilies, *bl l. m. b.* impr. by Denham, — *5. Congus*
  1572
1647 Marbecke's concordance to the Bible, *b. l.* impr. by — *4. Brander*
  Grafton, 1550
1648 Vincentius fuper pfalterium, *bl. l. m. g. l.* per Let- *5.10. Nicol*
  tou, 1481
1649 The judycyall, of Urynes, *bl. l.* 1526, and 1 more — *5.—*
1650 Gower de confeffione Amantis, *bl. l.* impr. by Ber- — *15. Jutat*
  thelet, 1532
1651 The woorkes of Boccas, in verfe, *bl. l.* imperfect, — *17. Fux.*
  1494
1652 The greate herball, *bl. l. m. g. l.* impr. by Kynge, *1. 1.— Nicol*
  1561
1653 The actis and conftitutionis of the realme of Scot- *1.16. Dr Hunter*
  land, maid in parliamentis, *bl. l. m. g. l.* impren-
  tit at Edinb. be Lekprewik, 1566
1654 An abridgment of the ftatutes, by Littleton, *bl. l,* *1.3.—*
  m, b, printed by Lettou and Machlinia, about
  1841
1655 The year-book, *b, l, m, b,* 1522, and ditto, 1533, — *15. Williams*
  impr. by Redman
1656 The year-book for the 34th year of Henry the 6th, *1. 18 —*
  b, l, m, g, l, printed by Maclyn
1657 The boke of the noble kyng Arthur *bl, l,* imperfect, *1. — Nicol*
  empr. by Wynkyn de Worde, 1498
1658 The noble experyence of the vertuous handy warke — *16.6 Utt*
  of furgeri, *bl, l,* imperf. 1525. The greate Herball, *b, l,* imperf.
1659 The year-boke, for the 37th year of Henry the 6th, *1.—.—*
  ditto, for the 19th year of Henry the 7th, by
  Pynfon, and part of Raftell's chronicle
1660 Two Arnold's chronicle, or cuftoms of London, *1.—. Thans*
  imperf. *b, l,*

2.13. — 1661 The ryal boke, for a kyng, *b, l,* imperf. printed by Caxton, 1483. Politick admonitions and obfervations fit for great men to perufe, *bl, l,* imperf. printed by Caxton

2.3. — 1662 Two poly chronicon's, *b, l,* imperf. emprentyd by Caxton, 1482

4.6. — 1663 The prouffytable boke for manes foule and right comfortable to the body, and fpecyally in adverfitye and trybulacyon, whiche boke is calle the chaftyfing of Goddes chyldern ; emprentyd by me William Caxton

3.3. — 1664 The lyf of Cryft, taken from Bonaventure, in confutation of the Lollards, in feaven parts, with a treatyce of the facrament, empr. by Caxton

5.10. — 1665 The boke of Jafon, *m. b.* empr. by Caxton

4.4. — 1666 A lytyll treatife of the arte and crafte to know well to dye, *m, b,* empr. by Caxton, 1490

4.18. — 1667 The fiege of Troye, *bl, l,* impr. by Caxton, 1490

4.6. — 1668 Boecius do confolacione philofophie, *bl, l, m, g, l,* by Cax on

5.15.6 — 1669 The poly chronicon, *bl, l, m, g, l,* empr. by Caxton, 1482

9.15. — 1670 Legenda aurea, or the golden legende, *bl, l, m, g, l,* Caxton, *The Prologue MS* 1493

— *.17.* — 1671 The booke of Common Prayer, *bl, l, g, l,* very rare, Lond impr. by Jugge, 1558

1.3 — 1672 La fanfte Bible, bien anvers, par Martin Lempereur, 1534

3.3. — 1673 The Holy Bible, 2 vols *bl, l, c, t, g, l,* impr. by Barker, 1585

7.15. — 1674 Mr. Ratcliffe's MSS. catalogues, of the rare old black letter, and other curious and uncommon books, 4 vols.

1.4. — 1675 Julii Cæfaris Vita & Res Geftæ cum Medallis, 1563, and 4 more.

F I N I S.